TABLE OF CONTENTS

ABBREVIATIONS AND ACRONYMS

A&A	Acquisition and Assistance
ADB	African Development Bank
ADF	Agence Française de Développement
AEG	Mali Accelerated Economic Growth
AGRA	Alliance for a Green Revolution in Africa
AOPP	Association des Organisations Professionnelles Paysannes
APCAM	Permanent Assembly of Malian Agricultural Chambers
ATN	Assistance Technique Nationale
BFS	Bureau of Food Security
BNDA	Banque Nationale de Developement Agricole
CAADP	Comprehensive Africa Agriculture Development Program
CDC	Centers for Disease Control
CGIAR	Consultative Group on International Agricultural Research
CLDP	Commercial Law Development Program
CMAM	Community Management of Acute Malnutrition
CNOP	Coordination Nationale des Organisations Paysannes
CPS	Cellule de Planification et de Statistique
CRSP	Collaborative Research Support Program
CSCOM	Centre de Santé Communautaire
DCA	Development Credit Alliance
DHS	Demographic and Health Surveys
DOD	Department of Defense
ECOWAS	Economic Community of West African States
FSN	Foreign Service National
FSO	Foreign Service Officer
EGAT	Economic Growth, Agriculture, and Trade
EMOP	Enquete Modulaire Permanent aupres des Menages
ENA	Essential Nutrition Actions
EU	European Union
FAO	Food and Agriculture Organization
FNAA	National Fund for Agricultural Support
FTF	Feed the Future
FTFS	Feed the Future Strategy
GDP	Gross Domestic Product
GHI	Global Health Initiative
GIS	Geographic Information System
GIZ	Deutsche Gesellschaft für Internationale Zusammenarbeit (formerly GTZ)
GOM	Government of Mali
Gov/Com	Governance & Communications
ICRISAT	International Crops Research Institute for the Semi-Arid Tropics
IEC	Information, Education and Communication
IER	Institut d'Economie Rurale
IFAD	International Fund for Agricultural Development
IFDC	International Fertilizer Development Center
IFPRI	International Food Policy Research Institute
IICEM	Initiative Integrée de Croissance Economique au Mali
ILRI	International Livestock Research Institute
IMF	International Monetary Fund

INSTAT	Institut International National de la Statistique
INTSORMIL	Sorghum and Millet Collaborative Research Support Program CRSP
IP	Implementing Partners
IPCC	Intergovernmental Panel on Climate Change
IPM	Integrated Pest Management
IPR	Institute Polytechnique Rurale
IR	Intermediate Result
KFW	Kreditanstalt für Wiederaufbau
LSMS-ISA	Living Standards Management Study – Integrated Surveys on Agriculture
MAM	Moderate Acute Malnutrition
MCC	Millennium Challenge Corporation
MCA	Millennium Challenge Account
MDG	Millennium Development Goal
M&E	Monitoring & Evaluation
MEAS	Modernizing Extension and Advisory Services Project
MENOR	Monitoring Externe National Oriente vers les Resultats
MSU	Michigan State University
MYAP	Multi-Year Assistance Program
NAPA	National Action Plan for Adaptation to Climate Change
NERICA	New Rice for Africa
NGO	Non-Governmental Organization
NIH	National Institute of Health
NRM	Natural Resource Management
OIC	Organization of Islamic Conferences
OMA	Observatoire des Marchés Agricoles
ON	Office du Niger
ORS	Oral Rehydration Salts
PAPAM	Projet d'Accroissement de la Productivité Agricole au Mali
PIR	Portfolio Implementation Review
PMP	Performance Management Plan
PNIP-SA	Priority Investment in the Sector of Agriculture of Mali
PNISA	National Plan for Investment in the Agriculture Sector
PRODESS II	Programme d'Investissement Secteur Santé II
PTF	Technical and Financial Partner
RGPH	Population and Household Census
SSBCC	Social and Behavior Change Communication
SME	Small and Medium Enterprise
SMS	Short Message Service
SPS	Sanitary and Phytosanitary
SUN	Scaling Up Nutrition
SWAp	Sector-Wide Approach
UNICEF	United Nations Children's Fund
USDA	United States Department of Agriculture
USG	United States Government
USGS	U.S. Geological Survey
VAD	Vitamin A Deficiency
WAEMU	West Africa Economic and Monetary Union
WASA	West Africa Seed Alliance
WHO	World Health Organization

I. INTRODUCTION

The Government of Mali's vision for the peaceful and prosperous future of the country depends on catalyzing an underdeveloped agricultural sector to fill its potential in stimulating broad-based economic growth and nourishing its population. According to the most recent census, 80 percent of Mali's population is under 24 years old and is increasingly migrating to the cities in search of better opportunities. Most employment opportunities will lie in the rural sector in the immediate future, however. The United States Government (USG) /Mali's Feed the Future (FTF) strategy seeks to launch a new generation of rural entrepreneurs through developing sustainable agricultural and health systems, utilizing technology and knowledge, and by building institutional capacity that will spur a vibrant private sector-led approach to achieve economic and food security. To do so, USG /Mali will build on the successes of its historic investments in agriculture and health; leverage the wealth of bilateral and multilateral donors that invest annually in Mali, and target interventions that are the most critical in transforming subsistence farming into an economic opportunity for Mali's youthful population. Its FTF strategy will commit mission resources across all sectors — education, health, governance, and economic growth — and from USG partners in the Department of State, Millennium Challenge Corporation (MCC), U.S. Department of Agriculture (USDA), and Department of Commerce to provide key interventions that unlock FTF potential.

In five years, USG/Mali will build the following attributes into FTF target areas:

- Sustainable market linkages.
- Systems to access technology and knowledge about agriculture and nutrition.
- Policies that largely support agricultural development.
- Sufficient farm-community based infrastructure.
- Local government leadership addressing community priorities in health and agriculture.
- Human capacity that understands agriculture as an income generating opportunity.
- Community leaders and mothers that understand the basics of child-hood nutrition.

Embracing the Feed the Future initiative principles of selectivity, focus, country-led programming, and coordination with other investors, USG will invest strategically to achieve measurable and sustainable outcomes in three agricultural value chains and in children's nutrition levels in three regions of Mali. It will strengthen priority value chains at points where they are most constrained; adapt technologies to local conditions; and enhance the ability of public and private delivery, extension and advisory services to disseminate information to Malian agricultural producers, processors and other players in the value chain. FTF will address high levels of nutritional deficiency by delivering a set of high impact, evidence-based interventions focused on messages delivered through behavior change communication techniques to improve care practices and dietary diversity, combined with efforts to strengthen nutrition service delivery systems. USG/Mali will improve the enabling environment for agricultural growth, food security, and nutrition by empowering selected public and private institutions at the local and national level to plan, develop, implement and monitor agricultural and food security strategies, including resolving land use conflicts. USG/Mali will use an evidence-based approach to engage the Government of Mali (GOM) in policy debates leading to meaningful change. Finally, and as the key to achieving long term sustainability, it will build capacity in education and research, including technical training and degree programs, to ensure that new technologies and best practices are integrated into value chain strengthening, and to ensure that a pipeline of new innovations — and personnel – will continue to augment Mali's agricultural sector.

Mali is poised for change and presents a prime opportunity for a return on development investment. It has one of the fastest growing economies in Africa with an average national growth rate of 5.4 percent annually over the past decade, and has recently undertaken key investment reforms that make it easier for entrepreneurs to establish and conduct business. USG /Mali and other development investors have demonstrated successful models and approaches to increase agriculture production and income, and have already developed technologies such as improved seeds that are poised for wider adoption and usage with new private and government partners. Paved roads now connect the major cities, with improved feeder roads evident in the most populated parts of the county. Mali's status as a largely peaceful country has enabled it to take advantage of the unfortunate fallout from regional conflicts. The GOM has demonstrated its full commitment to agriculture and health through its budgetary allocations and its leadership of the very active donor and partner community, the majority of which prioritize agriculture and infrastructure investments in line with GOM goals. Mali, however, remains near the bottom among all countries in economic and human development measures and has a significant need of effective development assistance, including increasing peace and security in the northern desert area.

<u>Selection of Priority Value Chains</u>

Through an analysis of poverty, nutrition and vulnerability; potential market demand; multiplier effects of potential investments; and through consultation with the GOM, donors, private sector actors, and NGOs, USG/Mali selected three value chains for investment under Feed the Future:

- **Millet and sorghum for food security and poverty reduction.** Intensifying production of this crop grown by 75 percent of Mali's farmers will increase household security and buffer climatic changes while increasing the supply of this important staple for some of Mali's most vulnerable. Working with entrepreneurs to build on growing urban demand for high quality processed products and livestock feed will further generate income across the economic spectrum.

- **Rice for growth in household incomes and food security.** Better water management, storage and uptake of improved technologies in smallholder rice production systems, combined with adopting voluntary quality standards and private sector investments will increase food supply and incomes at the local level, substitute for expensive imports, and potentially spur regional exports.

- **Livestock for growth in household incomes, nutrition and for national gross domestic product (GDP) growth.** Improving livestock nutrition and health through expanded access to watering points and more sustainable pasture management will increase the potential off-take rate and household incomes, while also boosting milk production. Women will enhance their opportunities to benefit from small-scale dairy activities and increase the availability of animal products.

- **Investments for improved nutrition.** In response to extensive consultations, a landscape analysis of existing public and private sector efforts to address chronic levels of stunting and wasting, and an analysis of comparative advantages was conducted. USG/Mali will invest in preventive services conducted through social and behavior change and efforts to strengthen the nutrition service delivery system as the core of the strategy's nutrition interventions.

- **Social and behavior change.** Substantial investments will be made to provide education and counseling around critical health and nutrition behaviors. FTF will use a "no missed opportunities" approach, using both traditional health and non-traditional platforms such as agriculture and financial service agents to communicate behavior change messages to people where they work or live.

- **Facility and community-based prevention and care.** Community mobilization and health service strengthening activities will continue to augment prevention services and ensure that high quality treatment for nutrition-related illness is available and accessible. Through the Global Health Initiative (GHI), USG/Mali will continue to reduce causes of malnutrition by supporting the prevention and treatment of childhood illnesses, ante- and post-natal care, healthy timing and spacing of pregnancies, HIV/AIDS prevention and care, and human resource development including local governance capacity-building.

- **Geographic targeting and beneficiaries.** To focus investments for maximum impact, USG/Mali will concentrate its interventions in 143 targeted communes, comprised of 3.15 million people, in three of Mali's eight regions – Sikasso, Mopti and Timbuktu — and the two communities in the Millennium Challenge Corporation intervention zones in the Alatona region of Segou. Target areas were primarily selected on their agricultural production potential and nutrition indicators, but also on population size, current USG programming, other donor activity, physical accessibility, and safety and security issues.

Technological Advancement

Education and Training: Financially support educational and research institutions, link extension and health services to these institutions, and support several research partnerships with U.S. universities and international research centers.

Research & Dissemination: Strengthen government and private sector systems to deliver maternal, child and reproductive health services, including nutrition; and strengthen GOM and agribusiness agricultural extension services through training, technical expertise, and linkages to central and community governments.

Value Chain Development

Markets and Trade Development: Build capacity among producers, millers, processors, and marketers to more efficiently manage their resources and add value to the goods that they produce. Target interventions for women and youth in order to build economic inclusiveness, and to develop economic networks among these groups.

Infrastructure: Construct storage facilities to reduce post-harvest grain losses and take advantage of better price points; build water management structures and small-scale irrigation systems to increase lowland rice production; construct watering holes to improve livestock health.

Credit and Finance: Improve agricultural banking and credit management capacities; work with existing financial institutions to establish credit guarantees for agricultural loans; integrate delivery of health education and behavior change messages into credit service platforms.

Enabling Environment

Policy / Enabling Environment: Assist the GOM to develop the systems, capacity, and structures to coordinate government, donor, civil society, and private sector support for FTF implementation. Alongside other donors, advocate for policy changes crucial to enabling agriculture and business, such as fertilizer and seed policy; and support the GOM to enact and enforce industrial food-based fortification legislation. Provide technical assistance to communities to help manage communal resources and leverage resources for their farming community, and strengthen local land commissions to demarcate land under customary law and foster community-based pasture land management in target communes. The decentralized systems will take more responsible management roles and develop collaborations and partnerships with key actors. As part of USG's support to the new GOM 10-year health strategy currently underway, they will promote nutrition as an elevated, cross-cutting issue in the GOM and support fortification policies for staple foods and supplements.

Monitoring and Evaluation Systems Development and Strengthening: Invest with other donors in the Living Standards Measurement Survey (LSMS-ISA), and support the Demographic and Health Survey to oversample in FTF intervention zones in order to establish a baseline.

<u>Nutrition</u>

Nutrition System Strengthening: Strengthen service delivery of maternal, child and reproductive health services, including nutrition services; and provide technical assistance to strengthen and support the health information and logistics management systems. Launch a Social Behavioral Change Communication (SBCC) and Social Marketing program that will encompass all SBCC under GHI and FTF.

2. DEVELOPMENT CHALLENGES AND OPPORTUNITIES

2.1 DEVELOPMENT CHALLENGES

Mali, an established, largely peaceful democracy, is poised for change. Its population is demonstrating its desire for new economic opportunity by beginning a migration to the cities. However, it is the rural agriculture sector that holds the greatest promise for spurring broad-based economic growth and livelihood development. Around 80 percent of the population still depends on agriculture for their livelihoods. Although much of the country is arid with only fair soil, the Niger River provides a rich base for agricultural development across multiple regions while the southern region is a lush subtropical climate, making it an ideal location for diversified agricultural products and livestock. Recent localized successes in agricultural intensification and marketing demonstrate that with improved technologies, better water management, sustainable agricultural practices, local community engagement and an enhanced enabling environment, Mali's agricultural potential can be fully realized to feed its population, generate economic growth, and jumpstart regional trade.

Despite being considered generally food secure year to year, Mali has high rates of malnutrition, which contribute to poor health status and diminished economic productivity, among other detriments. Malian diets are cereal-based and have little diversity in terms of fruits and vegetables or sources of animal protein. The social dynamics of gender and income distribution in the household, low educational attainment, cultural norms, and access to and use of health services all contribute to lowered health and nutritional status. Increased recognition of the nutrition problem within the Government of Mali, however, has resulted in a renewed commitment to address nutrition intersectorally, led from a high-level coordination body housed in the Prime Minister's office. This represents a promising signal from the Government of Mali that they are serious about addressing malnutrition. USG/Mali is well-positioned to be a leading partner with the government in this effort.

2.2 POVERTY-ECONOMIC SITUATION AND DEMOGRAPHICS

Mali is one of the fastest growing economies in Africa with an average national GDP growth rate of 5.4 percent annually over the past decade. The country has made significant progress toward achieving the

Millennium Development Goals (MDG) with reductions in the number of people living on less than a dollar a day from 86 percent in 1994 to 51 percent in 2006, and rates of underweight children decreasing from 40 to 27 percent between 2001 and 2006[1,2]. Poverty, measured by the cost of basic necessities, fell by eight percentage points between 2001 (55.6 percent) and 2006 (47.4 percent), though with notable regional disparities and rising urban poverty due to unemployment and rural exodus[3]. The number of mobile phone subscribers has risen significantly from a little under 3,000 in 1997 to over 3.7 million in 2008, and the percentage of paved roads has doubled over the last 20 years[4,5].

Despite this progress, Mali remains in position 160 of 169 countries on the Human Development Index (HDI) with over 51 percent of the population living on less than $1.25 per day and literacy rates among the lowest in the world at 26 percent[6]. It possesses one of the highest fertility rates in the world with 6.6 children per woman, leading to a 3.6 percent annual population growth rate and an unusually large, youthful population—80 percent of Malians are under the age of 24[7,8,9]. The population remains 70 percent rural, though urban migration is rapid and Bamako is estimated to be the fastest growing Sub-Saharan city. Only around 12 percent of all women are employed in the formal sector and they account for a little over 26 percent of all salaried employees[10].

The Government of Mali is taking strides to address deficiencies in the social and economic spheres by reaching out to its partners and adopting a cooperative approach to development. While gold and mineral exports play a large part in Mali's GDP growth rate, the agricultural sector, upon which over 80 percent of the population depends, contributes 34 percent of the nation's GDP. The 2007-08 food crisis forced the GOM to reexamine the centrality of agriculture to food security and broad-based economic growth, and encouraged it to partner with a host of international organizations to effect positive change in its rural economy. Healthcare is a national priority and the government is implementing a 10-year social and healthcare program that is now being evaluated. Substantial progress has been made in education, especially primary school gross enrollment, which was 80 percent in 2009.[11] The GOM made a strong commitment to decentralize its governance structure ten years ago. Progress has been made in transferring resources and in empowering communes to make decisions; real power and access to revenue lies in the hands of local decision-makers in education, for example, but progress varies by sector.

2.3 NUTRITION

Undernutrition rates remain high in Mali with 38 percent of children (1.1 million children chronically undernourished or stunted, a figure virtually unchanged over the last ten years.[12] Although the rates of underweight children have dropped in recent years, acute malnutrition rates, or the proportion of wasted children, have actually increased to over 15 percent, well above the World Health Organization (WHO) emergency threshold[13]. Anemia, due to iron deficiency as well as malaria and helminth

---

[1] World Bank 2010.
[2] UNICEF 2010.
[3] IMF 2010.
[4] CIA World Factbook 2001, 2011. Accessed 3/22/11.
[5] http://www.indexmundi.com/facts/mali/roads. Accessed 3/22/11.
[6] UNDP/Human Development Index, 2010.
[7] DHS, 2006.
[8] World Bank 2010.
[9] World Bank 2010.
[10] Sida. *Towards Gender Equality in Mali*. March 2004.
[11] GOM Ministry of Education, 2009/2010.
[12] DHS 2006.
[13] Demographic Health Survey (DHS) 2001 and DHS 2006.

infections, affects over 80 percent of children at a national level with this figure exceeding 90 percent in some regions (e.g., Sikasso). The impacts of childhood anemia manifest themselves later in life by causing an average 2.5 percent drop in wages as a child reaches adulthood.[14] Despite iodized salt being available in 79 percent of all areas, the latest data available shows that 34 percent of the population is iodine deficient[15,16]. In addition to physical and cognitive manifestations, these micronutrient deficiencies contribute to an estimated annual GDP loss of $235 million due to losses in productivity.[17]

Low access to quality health, nutrition and family planning services and significant gender inequities present major challenges to maternal and child health outcomes. The first 1,000 days of a child's life, from their conception until they reach 24 months of age, is the most critical part of their physical and mental development. Achieving positive future outcomes is hampered by the number of undernourished women and by high anemia rates regardless of geographic location or income status. Twenty-two percent of women also have children less than two years apart, further entrenching undernutrition.[18,19] Family planning services are critical to prolonging the birth interval; the USG will support the provision of complementary services in FTF target areas where possible. Poverty is also correlated with chronic undernutrition in Mali. Forty-four percent of children in the lowest economic quintile suffer from stunting compared to 13 percent in the highest quintile. Local studies demonstrate, however, that increased incomes and agricultural production are not sufficient by themselves to improve nutritional outcomes.[20] To address the complexity of nutrition outcomes, the GOM is committed to developing multisectoral programs that address access to modern healthcare practices and more strongly link to the healthcare system to improve overall dietary intake and disease status.

2.4 AGRICULTURAL PRODUCTIVITY

Mali's agricultural productivity significantly varies across regions, but common attributes are low productivity and high post-harvest losses. Crop yields in Mali are lower than averages in Africa and a significant percentage of cereal crops are lost before they reach market[21]. Even though microfinance is well-established in Mali, credit at a price and scale to enable farmers to purchase improved inputs is constrained. Dissemination and outreach to farmers on best practices in herding or cultivation techniques and new technologies has been poor. Market information and market access in general, is limited by poor infrastructure and gaps in the value chains. Agricultural institutions have an aging workforce, and an inadequate capacity and funding to train new generations of agricultural specialists or to deliver technical assistance to farmers in the field. The lack of security to land titles and opaque land administration has also reduced the incentive for investment in inputs and new technologies.

Climactic and geographic factors also constrain agricultural productivity on a regional basis. Mali is a very large and diverse country with a wide variety of climate zones among its regions, from the subtropical south to the arid deserts of the north, with corresponding high spatial and temporal rainfall variability. High evapo-transpiration rates mean that maintaining a proper amount of soil moisture is a key challenge

---

[14] Horton S and Ross J. 2003. The Economics of Iron Deficiency. Food Policy 28:517-5.

[15] DHS 2006.

[16] Kibambe N et al. Projet Thyromobil en Afrique de l'Ouest (première phase). Rapport final. [Thyromobil project in West Africa (first phase). Final report.] Lomé, Conseil International de Lutte contre les Troubles Dus à la Carence en Iode, 2000. Ref 2535

[17] UNICEF and the Micronutrient Initiative. 2004. Vitamin and Mineral Deficiency: A Global Progress Report.

[18] DHS 2006.

[19] Int J Gynaecol Obstet. 2005 Apr;89 Suppl 1:S7-24. Epub 2005 Jan 26. Effects of preceding birth intervals on neonatal, infant and under-five years mortality and nutritional status in developing countries: evidence from the demographic and health surveys.

[20] *From Agriculture to Nutrition: Pathways, Synergies, and Outcomes.* World Bank 2007.

[21] FAO 1997.

to realize improved rangeland productivity and rain-fed crop production[22]. Mali has 45.9 million hectares of land suitable for agricultural use, of which 11.5 percent is cultivable[23]. Only 325,000 hectares of Mali's cultivated areas have irrigation structures in place, with around one-third of this total having full water control[24]. At present, the GOM possesses little capacity to respond to the challenges of climate change in the agricultural sector, despite the existence of several structures that deal with climate change issues (e.g., meteorological stations, research institutions, climate change-related issues focal points, and an inter-ministerial climate change committee). In order for climate change solutions to be appropriately mainstreamed into government ministries and projects, these climate change-related bodies will require additional capacity building, including training in appropriate methodologies for vulnerability assessments, model generations, analysis and use of data.

Although low productivity currently characterizes the agricultural sector, several development opportunities exist that can boost agricultural production, raise household incomes, and deliver improved nutritional outcomes to citizens. Yields can be increased by encouraging the adoption of improved seeds, fertilizer, and best agricultural production practices, including water management systems. Post-harvest practices can be improved, including storage. Processing activities will create demand for raw materials that feed into new product formulations, while a focus on building the capacity of traders and aggregators with an emphasis on standards and quality will build closer ties between staple crop farmers and value-added processors. Smallholders and processors alike can benefit from training on marketing activities and from the implementation of a consistent grading and measures system to guide product quality. Expanding access to short- and medium-term credit and improving market information systems underpin all efforts to increase agricultural productivity. Involving marginalized groups like women and youth in the agricultural system to a greater extent will create a larger base of labor with which to mobilize for agricultural initiatives.

2.5 CROSS-CUTTING ISSUES

Gender

Women have a great potential to contribute to, and benefit from, agricultural productivity and nutrition improvements. At the national level, Mali has established some important legal underpinnings for the promotion of gender equality and human rights. In practice, however, there are considerable social, economic, and institutional barriers. Men are considered the heads of households and the managers of farm activities, and consequently women have limited control over household income and restricted access to other means of production such as equipment, raw material, and technology. Customary land tenure strongly limits women's access to agricultural land. Women received less than 1 percent of the total amount of credit dispensed between 1990 and 1995 and must normally form associations as a prerequisite to accessing credit[25]. Social norms burden women with responsibility for very labor-intensive domestic and agricultural daily responsibilities with little personal payoff.

Despite the low social and economic standing of women in Malian society, opportunities exist to reduce gender disparities and secure improved outcomes for women and their families. Women are active in several areas in the agricultural sphere, particularly in rice cultivation and processing activities, which are areas ripe for investment. Lowland rice cultivation, rice and grains processing, small ruminants farming, and artisanal food production are activities that are already predominantly managed by Malian women. Improving access to credit, adult literacy programs, technical training, and nutritional information can

---

[22] MSU 2011.
[23] GOM *Yields of the Ag. Sector*, October 2009.
[24] MSU 2011.
[25] Rosander, Eva Evers 2004 Towards Gender Equality in Mali. Netherlands: Sida.

assist women and their communities. Strong women's agricultural cooperatives that are already established in many communities attest to the ability of women to organize themselves as economic and social actors. They can also serve as platforms through which women can receive training and assistance in the economic and nutrition spheres in order to improve family outcomes. Malian women can be supported in several areas, most significantly through policy change, training, supporting the creation of productive associations, and improving access to inputs and services. An important note to consider, however, is that interventions must take place within the local community, as women are often prohibited from traveling beyond their immediate surroundings due to traditional gender perceptions and time burdens.

Climate Change

Mali is projected to be one of the countries most affected by climate change, but the present models do not definitively predict how the change will occur. Although the National Action Plan for Adaptation to Climate Change (NAPA), elaborated in 2007, foresees an increase in temperature and a change in rainfall patterns towards less rainfall and more extreme events, the different models used in the Intergovernmental Panel on Climate Change's (IPCC) fourth Assessment Report reveal a very different scenario, characterized by a shift from a dryer to a wetter Sahel. Drought and flooding are becoming more common in several areas, contributing to social tensions as people migrate out of areas affected by these events and into others. It is also highly probable that Mali, especially in the Saharan zone, will be affected by higher temperatures. A 3-4 C° degree increase in average temperature from 2080-2099 compared to 1980-1999 seems very likely for most African nations[26]. If these predictions are correct, the amount of arable land will effectively be reduced, leading to potential conflicts between pastoralists and farmers and, if combined with population growth models, will likely contribute to decreased food security. Despite the uncertainty in predicting future climatic changes, it is certain that Mali will face pressures to adapt to a changing climate. Engagement with local partners, including with the Ministry of Environment and Sanitation and the Ministry of Agriculture at the national level and with research centers at the local and international levels, is essential to foster a positive policy environment to advocate for environmentally sustainable interventions. For this reason, some crops like millet and sorghum assume a high priority for development by the GOM because of their tolerance to drought. Other actions like water management, improved and drought-resistant seed varieties and intercropping contribute to climate change adaptation and are also high priorities as expressed in the National Plan of Priority Investment in the Sector of Agriculture of Mali (PNIP-SA), the GOM's five-year agricultural development policy.

Business Environment

As indicated in the World Bank's Doing Business 2011 report (see Annex A), Mali has recent and impressive gains in reforming the business environment and now requires fewer procedures and time spent on procedures than the regional averages in several key areas. Several challenges confront business owners, however, including an inadequate financial system, underdeveloped agricultural infrastructure, and almost non-existent business support services. Many businesses have difficulty in attracting capital and banks do not favor agricultural loans because of a high default rate among agricultural enterprises and a lack of risk assessment tools. Several opportunities exist to further improve the business climate in partnership with the Government and private sector associations. GOM recently launched a transparent business registry. It also erected a mechanism, the National Fund for Agricultural Support (FNAA), to increase access to credit and financial services, and reduce bank

---

[26] Appréciation des Impacts des Changements Climatiques sur les Programmes de Développement de la Coopération Danoise au Mali.

interest rates to agricultural producers. Coordinated policy advocacy with donor coordination groups can be leveraged to bring a host of issues to the attention of policy-makers in the GOM. Mali's group of technical and financial partners (PTF) is very active in several areas such as advocating for more equitable input subsidies and harmonizing national standards with regional and international ones. The Department of Commerce and the Department of State are already active in policy advocacy in several issues, including building an intellectual property rights regime and supporting biotechnology policy.

2.6 GOVERNMENT OF MALI PRIORITIES

The government's strong commitment to agriculture and its willingness to engage a wide variety of partners in its development present a real opportunity for agricultural transformation as a means of securing broad-based economic growth. GOM is preparing a 10-year National Plan for Investment in the Agriculture Sector (PNISA) to transition towards a sector-wide approach. In the interim, it has developed the CAADP (Comprehensive Africa Agriculture Development Program) PNIP-SA, a five-year country investment plan for agricultural development. The PNIP-SA provides a blueprint for agricultural development during the 2011-2015 timeframe. It focuses on strategic investments in five value chains: rice, maize, millet and sorghum, inland fisheries, and livestock products (both meat and dairy) with the goal of achieving a 6 percent annual agricultural GDP growth rate. Its objectives are to increase cereal, animal, and aquaculture production; improve the incomes of producers; and improve peoples' nutritional status. The GOM hopes to initially align various donor efforts around the priorities outlined in the PNIP-SA and, when completed, the entire PNISA, in order to move to a deeper sector-wide approach.[27] The GOM has exceeded the CAADP guideline of agricultural expenditures of 10 percent of GDP since 1995 and is averaging 12.8 percent annually since 2006[28]. All of the above government priorities are tied to establishing a greater degree of gender equity within Malian society. *La Politique Nationale Genre du Mali* includes 19 modes of intervention to improve gender equity including improving access to training, improving the profitability of women's agricultural work and of informal enterprises, and increasing support services to women in agriculture (e.g., finance, training, and agricultural techniques).

The GOM has identified nutrition as a priority in both the Ministry of Agriculture and the Ministry of Health, and is being highly innovative in linking the two sectors and ministries. The PNIP-SA contains a nutrition objective "to improve nutritional status of the population through Information, Education and Communication (IEC) activities." In addition, the Ministry of Health organized its first *Nutrition Forum* in June 2010 to raise nutrition as an inter-ministerial priority to be addressed by a concerted multisectoral effort. As a result of the meeting, the GOM established an inter-ministerial Nutrition Unit at the Prime Minister level to allow for greater collaboration. The Ministry of Health has also highlighted nutrition as a major contributor to positive maternal and child health outcomes in the Programme d'investissement secteur santé *II* (PRODESS II), the national health policy. The Prime Minister has expressed interest in becoming a Scaling Up Nutrition (SUN) partner country following the finalization of new health and poverty reduction strategies to be completed in December 2011.

USG/Mali is a member of the nutrition working group of the PRODESS II, which has responsibility for providing technical input and support to the GOM's next 10-year health strategy, and is active in the GOM/donor coordinating groups on rural development and agriculture.

2.7 DONOR COLLABORATION

Mali has an unusually well-organized donor coordination system. Over 30 donors and partners, fully committed to the principles of the Paris Declaration, currently invest in Mali. Most support agriculture,

---

[27] GOM, PNIP-SA 2010.
[28] GOM, *Yields of the Ag. Sector*, October 2009.

health, and rural development as a major part of their investments either in bilateral projects or in larger initiatives. Among major agricultural donors, USG and the World Bank apply a value chain approach to targeted products while the French, Canadians, and Dutch focus on institutional domestic institution capacity building, including producers' organizations, cooperatives, and decentralized agricultural administrations. Other major donors like the African Development Bank (ADB), the International Fund for Agricultural Development (IFAD), the Islamic Development Bank, and other Arab development funds collaborate on the broader agenda of rural development, particularly on rural infrastructure and the livestock sector. Access to credit is another important area where donors provide support. Donors such as the ADB, the Aga Khan Foundation, *Deutsche Gesellschaft für Internationale Zusammenarbeit* (GIZ), and the World Bank actively encourage decentralized Malian financial service and microfinance institutions to facilitate access to credit for rural producers and other private sector actors.

Within this context of multiple interventions, the donor community has agreed to align agriculture-related programming around the PNISA, currently under elaboration through a highly participatory process that will conclude before the end of 2011. In the interim, donors are leveraging work under the PNIP-SA, with current efforts aimed at supporting its key elements while addressing the identified challenges of climate change, infrastructure, managing surplus production, coordinating activities between the public and private sectors, risk management, access to credit, and sustainable management of natural resources.

In the context of health, USG is the largest donor to Mali and plays a significant role in donor collaboration and providing technical assistance to the Government of Mali. While USG does not provide basket funding in Mali, a complementary relationship exists where USG provides significant technical assistance to the government to appropriately govern and allocate basket resources through the sector-wide approaches (SWAp), which in Mali is known as the PRODESS. The evaluation and development of a new 10-year PRODESS is underway, and support to this strategic document is a priority of USG under the Global Health Initiative. Nutrition is an area where coordination has been historically weak. With the infusion of nutrition funding under FTF, however, USG will join UNICEF as a primary donor in this technical area. As such, the two agencies are in consultation to develop a Memorandum of Understanding to guide programming and coordination in the area of nutrition.

The USG is also an active member of the Private Sector, Health, Nutrition, Water and Sanitation, Education, and Governance Donor Coordination Groups. It will continue to play a key role in building dialogue among all GOM actors in Mali's agriculture, food security and nutrition sectors, including the Ministry of Agriculture, the Ministry of Livestock and Fisheries, the Ministry of Environment, the Ministry of Health, and the Food Security Commission.

Please see Annex F for a table describing donor activities in Mali and possible areas of collaboration.

2.8   LEVERAGING THE PRIVATE SECTOR

Growing the private sector in the areas of agriculture and health, specifically in the provision of inputs, knowledge services, transaction and aggregation, and advisory services will have transformative effects on social and economic development in Mali. Establishing and supporting private associations of producers is a key intervention. Currently, about ten large enterprises dominate the agro-food industry in Mali, including three flour mills, a brewery, and two large food and beverage companies. In addition, many informal small and micro-enterprises are engaged in the processing of cereals.

Though still fledgling enterprises, marketing agents and aggregators are beginning to appear, as are some input providers. Over 20 agri-distributors have been launched with support from the Bill & Melinda Gates Foundation. Many women's enterprises are concentrated in the informal private sector. The Law on Agriculture encourages the organization of private stakeholders working in agriculture. The Permanent Assembly of Malian Agricultural Chambers (APCAM), a private institution representing agro-related private stakeholders, provides producers' organizations with a platform for mutual consultations with other stakeholders such as input providers, transporters and exporters. APCAM and its nine Regional Agricultural Chambers participate in most agricultural policy discussions at the national and regional level, on a host of issues. APCAM plays a critical role in providing market information through the *Observatoire des Marchés Agricoles* (OMA). The national Co-ordination of Rural Producers' Organizations (CNOP) also represents various producers' organizations.

Private sector provision of health services in Mali is historically weak, but opportunities do exist for leveraging this important set of actors through social marketing and the commercial complementary food market. Opportunities exist to build on the success of social marketing programs to expand access of health commodities targeted intervention areas through the private sector. Some examples include oral rehydration salts (ORS) with zinc supplementation, point-of-use water treatment products, branded complementary food products, and other health commodities. Supply shortages of products produced by private sector actors are a concern to many Malians. Building capacity in large processors and with business associations to solidify production and distribution chains will reduce perceptions that such products are in short supply.

2.9   WHOLE OF GOVERNMENT COMPARATIVE ADVANTAGE

USG has the experience, network of relationships, and proven successes to contribute to the implementation of Feed the Future. USG built several agricultural research centers that continue to contribute to technology improvement; further aid is needed to disseminate these innovations. USG pioneered the value chain approach and gathered considerable expertise and knowledge both in linking components and in modes of intervention, tailored to different regions. As the largest health donor in Mali, USG already has significant existing investments in improving the supply and demand of health service utilization through health system strengthening, human resource development and facilitative supervision, community mobilization, social marketing of health commodities (e.g., water treatment kits and oral rehydration salts with zinc), and communication strategies to improve essential health actions including nutrition. USG has consistently strong relationships with the GOM, maintained through American staffing transitions by a strong cadre of Malian personnel who have immediate access to the highest levels of government. Increasingly, young Malians are turning to the U.S. for higher education and training opportunities; their presence in new enterprises as well as in government continues to build solid and effective relations between the two countries. USG/Mali can also leverage resources to build gender equity in Malian society, including a general Mission gender advisor, gender advisors for each technical team, and participation in a bi-weekly donor's coordinating committee on gender.

The Millennium Challenge Corporation (MCC) is active in the Alatona region of Segou where USG/Mali has agreed to partner with it on sustainability projects, including institutional strengthening of communes, building capacity among water user associations and farmer organizations, and land administration. MCC has a comparative advantage in large infrastructure and has developed large-scale systems to irrigate over 5,000 hectares, but it will not have sufficient time to strengthen the institutional reforms and capacity-building activities before its Compact ends in 2012. The creation of an institutional structure in which water users play a central role is essential to the sustainability of the Alatona irrigation infrastructures. The design of the Mali Compact included the creation of an institutional and organization structure that is autonomous and independent from the existing Office du Niger management structure. This structure operates and maintains the physical infrastructure and provides water services to the producers. The Alatona institutional structure is expected to sign a water contract with the Office du Niger to ensure water is provided to the main gate of the Alatona perimeter, thereby limiting the role of the Office du Niger to that of a water service provider. Building strong farmers' organizations is also necessary to sustain the Alatona project, but the present ones erected by MCC will be very inexperienced by the time the Compact expires. A risk exists that they may fail and the management of the perimeter revert to the classic Office du Niger model instead of the more robust model promoted by the MCC project. Finally, a well-managed land rights program can transform the Alatona region and have spillover effects for how a proper land administration regime can be rolled out to other agricultural areas.

This scheme must be correctly implemented, however, and the resources generated through the formalization of rights must lead to local development to provide an incentive to other areas. The first annual payment for land by the beneficiaries is not expected until 2011. This means that the bulk of the first annual payments for land will be made only in 2012, the year when the Compact ends. In these conditions, the USG needs to ensure that the post-Compact flow of revenues and the management of these revenues are done in a proper and transparent manner.

The U.S. Department of Agriculture (USDA) is also active in Mali at several levels. It has piloted a local purchasing program that organizes producer associations and expands market linkages in regions where multiple USG/Mali projects are active, including those in health and economic growth. The Multi-Year Assistance Program (MYAP) goals and objectives – to reduce food insecurity in targeted areas – will continue to complement the economic focus on increasing production, productivity, and marketing of rice, sorghum and millet, livestock, and fisheries. The USDA/McGovern Dole Food for Education Program supports school feeding program for over 34,000 school children and complementary activities such as improving school infrastructure, providing vitamin A and de-worming medication, and health and nutrition training[29]. The USDA Forest Service is working on reforestation in several locations, as it plays a critical role in addressing some of the challenges associated with climate change.

The USDA Food for Progress program focuses on value chain development and market competitiveness of sesame and fonio. This program will improve the livelihoods of smallholders and entrepreneurs with a particular focus on women. Finally, an USDA-funded International Science and Education competitive grants program is helping U.S.-based universities to internationalize their teaching, research, and extension programs. In Mali, this work is being conducted in conjunction with Sam Houston University to strengthen the core agricultural curriculum at the University of Segou and at the University of Bamako.

A high-level coordinating committee led by USAID/Mali and the Department of State prioritizes policy issues and develops interventions to improve the enabling environment, particularly in politically sensitive issues such as land administration, seed sector policy and biotechnology. Peace Corps has a Food Security volunteer division in Mali comprising sixty new volunteers that will support programs in areas such as agricultural SME development, natural resource management (NRM), health and nutrition, water and sanitation, and education. USG has embedded a senior advisor in the Peace Corps to help train and coordinate the volunteer corps. The Famine Early Warning Systems Network (FEWS NET), a USG-funded activity, is present in Mali and tracks the relationship of climate to hunger. Finally, the U.S. African Development Foundation focuses on grassroots associations, cooperatives, and businesses involved in the production, processing, and marketing of livestock; rice and dry season production; processing; and marketing, particularly in the Timbuktu region. Over 50 percent of its project participants and beneficiaries are women.

USG/Mali also leverages its regional ties with the USG/West Africa (WA) regional missions in Dakar and Accra, and with the USDA regional post in Dakar to conduct work on international trade facilitation,

---

[29] USDA 2010.

particularly among trade corridors that link Bamako with Dakar and Lomé. USG/WA has a major focus on expanding regional trade and together with USG/Mali will continue to look for regional integration links and realize efficiencies in regional Feed the Future programs to achieve a greater impact over the life of the strategy. USDA also manages some regional programs, including trainings on biosafety, sanitary and phytosanitary (SPS) issues, animal health, plant pests and climate change. The Department of Commerce under the Commercial Law Development Program (CLDP) is working in Mali to support an improved intellectually property rights regime, important for encouraging investment in the seed sector.

The Global Health Initiative, of which Mali is a part, systematically integrates health and nutrition activities across the USG. USG/Mali works hand in hand with its Centers for Disease Control (CDC) and National Institute of Health (NIH) partner agencies. A major focus of the GHI Mali strategy is supporting the development of the new 10-year health plan, PRODESS, ensuring that USG is coordinated with the GOM. USG partners also work closely with the GOM to strengthen maternal and child health services at the facility and community levels in 35 of the 59 districts of the country. In addition, the Office of Foreign Disaster Assistance (OFDA) has supported an assessment of Community-Based Management of Malnutrition (CMAM) activities in Mali and is currently co-funding a research study in Koulikoro to look at different treatment options for moderate acute malnutrition (MAM).

2.10   SUSTAINABILITY CHALLENGES

Demographic shifts present the greatest challenge to the effectiveness of interventions. Mali has one of the highest annual rates of population growth in the world at 3.6 percent; a risk exists that population growth will outstrip any gains in agricultural sector growth under Feed the Future. Rapid urbanization in Mali presents another challenge; as more Malians move to urban areas, interventions along the value chain must be structured in different ways to address the different problems that urban and rural dwellers face. Yet, urbanization is not just a challenge, as it can also present opportunities for value chain development, including a shift toward value-added processing, which could stimulate private sector agricultural growth just as it did in the U.S.

Several political factors may influence the success of FTF programming. 2012 is an election year for a new president, with the possible effects of a distracted administration and changes in policy. Given the importance of the two FTF sectors, health and agriculture, however, it seems unlikely that policy changes would be dramatic. As local governments increase their responsibilities and authorities under the continued commitment to decentralization, the labor pool of effective public leaders and administrators will be stretched. The continuing GOM policy of devolving authority from the central government to the regions injects an element of uncertainty regarding the balance between cooperating on new initiatives and strengthening internal capacity within the communes, particularly on issues of staffing and funding. Any uncertainty can be mitigated by supporting regional authorities, especially during the transition to a more decentralized system of governance.

Domestic policy concerns could trump economic ones, especially if commodity price shocks occur within the region. It is possible that a repeat of the spike in price of key agricultural commodities could spur export restrictions and handcuff regional trade for agricultural products. To overcome this obstacle, donors and other development partners in Mali can leverage their activities with each other and speak with a unified voice to make the GOM aware of the negative consequences of commodity export bans while managing commodity price spikes on a regional basis.

There are also certain external risks to the implementation of the Feed the Future strategy. The uncertainty surrounding how climate change will affect Mali is a significant sustainability challenge; it may affect investments in seed technology, systems of intensification, animal health, and land administration efforts. Building stronger local institutions will aid efforts to address climate change, as the regional authorities will be better placed to tailor programs for their specific situations instead of adopting a blanket approach that would be ineffective in a country as large and diverse as Mali. Regional political stability is an ongoing concern that that can have negative repercussions on economic growth throughout the sub-region, create barriers to trade, and negatively impact stability in the north of Mali.

3.   CORE INVESTMENT AREAS

The following section outlines the core investment areas of the Feed the Future strategy in Mali. On the basis of the analysis that has been conducted thus far, USG/Mali can expect the following over the next five years:[30]

Through Feed the Future in Mali, over the next five years:

- An estimated 556,000 vulnerable Malian women, children, and family members – mostly smallholder farmers – will receive targeted assistance to escape hunger and poverty.
- More than 255,000 children will be reached with services to improve their nutrition and prevent stunting and child mortality.
- Significant numbers of additional rural populations will achieve improved income and nutritional status from strategic policy and institutional reforms.

3.1   PRIMARY INVESTMENT AREAS

In conjunction with the GOM and development partners, USG commissioned a number of sectoral assessments, conducted extensive reviews of its experience in Mali to determine best practices, and consulted with a broad array of whole of government U.S. entities, development partners, and civil society groups to position its Feed the Future strategy along the four broad priority areas listed below (also shown in Figure 1):

- **Strengthen priority value chains** at points where they are most constrained; adapt technologies to local conditions; and enhance the ability of public and private delivery, extension and advisory services to disseminate information to Malian agricultural producers, processors and other players in the value chain.

- **Address high levels of nutritional deficiency** by delivering a set of high impact, evidence-based interventions focused on prevention messages around improving care practices and dietary diversity specific to the context in target areas, combined with efforts to strengthen nutrition service delivery systems.

- **Improve the enabling environment** for agricultural growth, food security and nutrition by empowering selected public and private institutions at the commune and national level to plan, develop, implement and monitor agricultural and food security strategies, including resolving land use conflicts. Using an evidence-based approach, engage the GOM in policy debates leading to meaningful change.

---

[30] These preliminary targets were estimated based on analysis at the time of strategy development using estimated budget levels and ex-ante cost-beneficiary ratios from previous agriculture and nutrition investments. Therefore, targets are subject to significant change based on availability of funds and the scope of specific activities designed. More precise targets will be developed through project design for specific Feed the Future activities.

- **Build education and research capacity**, including technical training and research-based degree programs, to ensure that new technologies and best practices are integrated into value chain strengthening, and to ensure a pipeline of new innovations—and personnel--will continue to augment Mali's agricultural sector.

Gender equity, natural resource management and climate change interventions will be integrated into each of the above primary investment areas. Gender analyses and environmental reviews (including climate change vulnerability assessments) will be conducted and integrated into new projects to allow researchers to identify not only the adaptation and resilience activities, but also the domains in which further research can be supported. Nutrition will be integrated into every phase of the Feed the Future strategy and all strategic decisions will feature a full complement of nutritional activities.

Figure 1. Mali Feed the Future Core Investment Areas

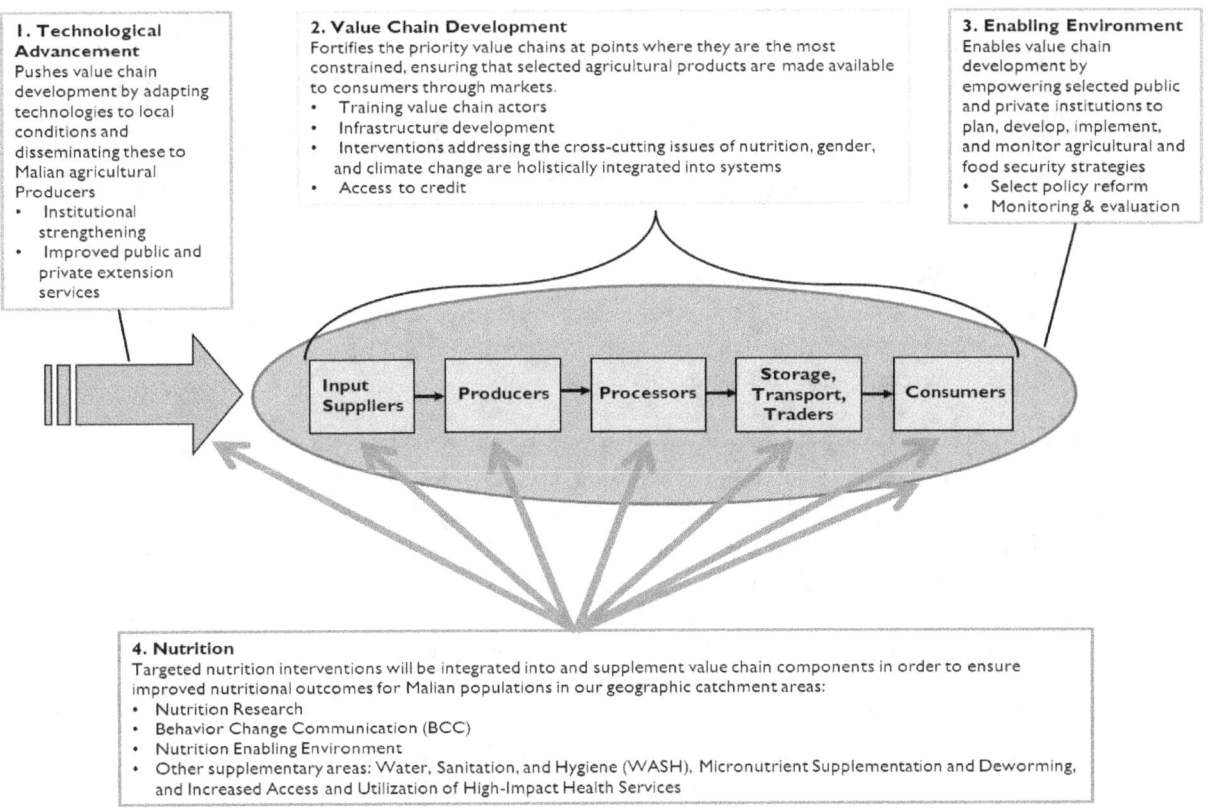

The USAID Forward initiative places a greater emphasis on building the capacity of local institutions than in the past. In line with the Paris Declaration, the partners that comprise the PTFs in the agricultural and health sectors have pledged to cooperate in a closer manner, particularly with the development of the major FTF, PAPAM, and AGRA Breadbasket agricultural and nutritional development strategies. USG/Mali is encouraging the GOM to lead this process and assume a greater ownership role over its agricultural development and nutrition programs. Within the scope of the PNIP-SA, USG/Mali will support local institutions that will be integral to its design, execution, monitoring, and evaluation in the 2011-2015 timeframe. The CPS is central to this process, as it is responsible for determining the cost of the PNIP-SA. Financial and technical assistance to the CPS will help the GOM with financial planning and donor coordination. To this end, USG/Mali already has commissioned a domestic resource cost analysis for the PNIP-SA and shared it with partners in the CPS to better understand the implications of the investments proposed within the PNIP-SA. USG/Mali has asked the Chief Financial Officer in the

USAID/Washington headquarters for assistance to appraise the capacity of GOM Ministry of Agriculture to receive direct support from FTF funds; a response is expected by the end of the year. In the meantime, USG/Mali has created a Mission-wide Local Capacity Development team that will develop tools to assess the capacity of local partners, including the government and private sector; FTF is this team's top priority. The results of the analyses conducted by these entities will direct USG/Mali FTF investments through the GOM and local institutions. USG/Mali will seek to provide assistance to private sector entities that have business plans aligned with the priorities outlined in the PNIP-SA.

3.1.1 Agriculture

USG/Mali used the GOM's PNIP-SA as a foundational document to guide the selection of value chains and interventions within those value chains. Further specificity was obtained by modifying a selection matrix originally developed by McKinsey & Company to determine a menu of interventions designed to increase nutritional status and incomes in Mali (Table 1). The matrix examined eight value chains: horticulture, corn, wheat, sorghum/millet, livestock, rice, poultry, and aquaculture. These value chains were evaluated across eight criteria: number of total beneficiaries, degree of market demand, effects on poverty reduction and vulnerability, intrinsic nutritional content, whether the product was a priority of the GOM, multiplier effects on other value chains, its effect on economic growth, and the presence of other donors working on that product. Additional input on value chain prioritization was sought from the Prime Minister and Ministry of Agriculture, private sector companies, the PTF, and representatives of the NGO community.

On the basis of the analytical framework and process described above, USG/Mali determined that sorghum/millet, rice, and livestock held the greatest potential to accomplish the objectives of securing a broad-based reduction in poverty, particularly among women, boosting agricultural GDP growth; and increasing nutritional outcomes for the most vulnerable.

USG/Mali has identified several analytic gaps and will address them during the activity planning stage, including analyses of the livestock value chain, a MicroCLIR agricultural enabling environment analysis, an extension and agricultural services assessment, a seed sector analysis, and a water assessment. The GOM does not analyze data that measures several key areas like how many farmers or households work in different agricultural areas and the amount of average household income. For this reason, it is difficult to establish targets in terms of number and type of beneficiaries, or how much they would benefit from Feed the Future interventions. USG will take a variety of approaches to collect and analyze data to establish targets, including by asking partners to establish a baseline for their target areas as a precursor to their value chain and nutrition strengthening work, through commissioning value chain analyses (including cost-benefit analyses and gender analyses), and working with the Ministry of Agriculture CPS to improve its data collection and analysis capabilities. The Living Standards Management Study – Integrated Surveys on Agriculture (LSMS-ISA), developed by the World Bank, will be a very effective tool to determine whether our interventions benefit the target areas, but initial data will not be published until 2013, limiting its use in establishing baselines for USG Feed the Future targets. Transitioning the *Monitoring Externe National Oriente vers les Resultats* (MENOR) approach supported by the Embassy of Sweden in the Institut National de la Statistique (INSTAT) to the Ministry of Agriculture Cellule de Planification et de Statistique (CPS) is another option for establishing a baseline and setting targets before USG interventions commence.

Table 1. Value Chain Decision Matrix

Criteria	Horti-culture	Corn	Wheat	Sorghum / Millet	Live-stock	Rice	Poultry	Fish / Aquaculture
1. Total beneficiaries	Low	Low	Low	**High**	**High**	**High**	**High**	Medium
2. Market demand	Low	**High**	Medium	**High**	**High**	**High**	**High**	**High**
3. Poverty reduction & vulnerability	Low	Medium	Low	**High**	**High**	**High**	**High**	Medium
4. Nutrition	**High**	Low	Medium	Medium	**Medium**	Low	**High**	**High**
5. GOM priority	**Yes**	**Yes**	No	**Yes**	**Yes**	**Yes**	No	**Yes**
6. Multiplier Effects	No	**Yes**	**Yes**	**Yes**	**Yes**	**Yes**	No	No
7. Economic growth	Low	Medium	Low	Medium	**High**	**High**	Medium	Medium
8. Donor Saturation	Medium	Low	Low	Low	**High**	**High**	Medium	Medium

The USG program has initiated assessments aimed at deepening its understanding of the effects that gender dynamics have on project activities and outcomes, and how its projects affect men and women differently, but acknowledges that it needs to collect more data about gender in the project design phase of Feed the Future. USG/Mali does not intend to conduct a separate gender analysis, but instead will integrate gender into every analysis that it conducts in the future to better capture the integrated nature of gender into Feed the Future programming. Some recent analytics include an operational study of the integration of gender into the USG program, including recommendations on the preparation and review of implementing partner work plans, a review of each USG project's knowledge and "handling" of gender in their activities, and project-specific recommendations. IICEM—USG's flagship and coordinating contract—is finalizing a gender analysis and action plan for the millet-sorghum value chain. The document follows the USG methodology developed in *Promoting Gender Equitable Opportunities in Agricultural Value Chains*, and will serve as a model of how the methodology can be applied to other value chains targeted by the FTF program. The observations and recommendations derived from these assessments inform the choices reflected in this strategy, and are cited throughout this document.

3.1.2 Nutrition

Preventing the onset of the disease-undernutrition cycle in the critical 1,000 day period from conception to a child's second birthday will have the greatest long-term impact on nutrition outcomes and on the overall level of productivity among the population. A set of high-impact, evidence-based interventions will be at the base of nutrition activities in the USG/Mali Feed the Future strategy.[31] The strategy will focus on using social and behavior change to promote preventive strategies in order to improve care practices and dietary diversity. These efforts will be combined with initiatives to strengthen nutrition service delivery systems. National-level policy advocacy and coordination with multiple ministries (e.g., Health, Agriculture) will serve as a platform with which to enact these changes. In addition, several opportunities exist that can boost nutritional outcomes in the context of a high-poverty environment. Poverty alleviation, particularly in rural areas, can be addressed with increasing agricultural productivity, diversifying crop production to reduce vulnerability, increasing access to water, and reducing post-harvest losses. These actions will improve access to resources, both in terms of food and income. As noted earlier, however, poverty alleviation by itself is an insufficient measure to secure positive nutritional outcomes. As a result, USG/Mali will use preventive, service delivery and policy-level platforms in conjunction with agriculture activities to ensure a comprehensive approach to nutrition in FTF target areas.

USG recognizes that gender is a very important causal factor in nutritional outcomes. Research shows that a mother's low educational attainment, limited control over household income, poor nutritional status, and little disposable time for breastfeeding or to prepare nutritious foods for her family are all factors that contribute to a poor household nutritional status. For example, USG is exploring the possibility of supporting the production and market development of one or several locally-made infant complementary foods in order to improve the distribution and affordability of such foods that are normally are too time-consuming to prepare at the household level.

Promote Social and Behavior Change Communication

Social and behavior change communication (SBCC) is at the core of USG/Mali Feed the Future interventions in nutrition and knowledge dissemination to improve diet quality and diversity, care practices and health outcomes. Critical behaviors affecting nutritional outcomes will be addressed through substantial investments in mass media, and through peer-to-peer education activities and counseling. A weak and overstretched extension infrastructure presents a major challenge to the promotion of behavior change at the individual, household, and community levels. As a result, USG/Mali will conduct formative research in advance of message development. It will use an innovative "no missed opportunities" approach oriented around the use of traditional and non-traditional platforms to deliver health messages, including agricultural groups and financial services. USG BCC messages will also address important gender-related nutritional constraints, and will target women and children, as well as heads-of-households and other male leaders with these messages. Such an inclusive communication approach should ensure that entire households and communities are engaged to actively promote gender equality and nutrition.

SBCC messages will be linked to interventions designed to address perceived barriers in the following subject areas: water quality and treatment, care and feeding during episodes of diarrhea, infant and young feeding practices, maternal nutrition, and dietary diversity.

---

[31] In 2008 the Lancet journal reviewed essential interventions with proven effects on maternal and child undernutrition and nutrition-related outcomes. These include "the promotion of breastfeeding; strategies to promote complementary feeding, with or without provision of food supplements; micronutrient interventions; general supportive strategies to improve family and community nutrition; and reduction of disease burden (promotion of hand washing and strategies to reduce the burden of malaria in pregnancy)." "What Works? Interventions for Maternal and Child Undernutrition and Survival," The Lancet, February 2008. Volume 371, Issue 9610.

Ongoing SBCC around other essential health actions in maternal and child health, reproductive health and HIV/AIDS prevention will complement these activities as a part of USG/Mali's broader health investments. All messages will conform to the Ministry of Health's nutrition policy and standards, thus ensuring the consistency of SBCC content and priorities with other projects and GOM programs.

<u>Strengthen Nutrition Service Delivery</u>

USG/Mali will work to strengthen host country health systems and community-based health activities. Emphasis will be given to preventive nutrition activities through the *Semaine d'Intensification des Activites Nutritionnelles* (SIAN), or Child Nutrition Weeks, that provide education and service delivery, including growth measurement and counseling, vitamin A supplementation, and diarrhea kits. The prevention and treatment of childhood illnesses, support to ante- and post-natal service delivery (such as anemia prevention and control through iron folate supplementation and education), and improvements to staff capacity (such as training and formative supervision) will continue as integral components to the nutrition activities in Feed the Future in conjunction with the Global Health Initiative. As part of the Best Action plan, which includes maternal and child health, family planning, and nutrition, additional efficiencies will be created through health facility and community programs. In collaboration with the Ministry of Health and the UNICEF, USG will work to ensure that quality nutrition rehabilitation services are available and provided for in cases of acute malnutrition.

3.2 SELECTED VALUE CHAIN ANALYSIS

One major issue that cuts across all value chains is how to overcome the barriers to adoption of agricultural best practices. Low literacy rates, underfunded GOM extension services, and remote distances between constituents make Mali a difficult environment in which to disseminate information about improved inputs, access to credit, and modern agricultural practices. A development hypothesis that has been advanced by several models is that if farmers are given technical assistance, access to credit, and can see the results in demonstration plots, then they will be able to market their products more efficiently and at a higher price, thus increasing the adoption of new techniques and technologies. All four models analyzed (IICEM, INTSORMIL, GREFA, and FASO KABA) have similar structures in that they provide inputs for the first two years of demonstration and work closely with extension agents.

The IICEM and GREFA models are of particular interest with regards to the selected value chains. In these models, farmers use producer organizations in order to enter into a credit guarantee mechanism for the first two years to purchase inputs. The farmer organizations receive training and are encouraged to establish savings accounts to purchase basic inputs such as seeds and fertilizer. During the first year, farmer organization field schools are established where farmers volunteer to be early adopters, receive technical assistance, organize field days, and disseminate their findings through the radio and television. During the second year, the farmers who participated in the first year of the program help extension agents train a new cohort of farmers for the program. In the third year, extension agents only provide monitoring services as the farmers engaged in the previous two years of the program train others on new techniques. This model also lends sustainability to the farmers' organizations because they are able to save more money with the surplus funds received from the crops marketed using improved inputs and modern agricultural practices.

<u>Millet & Sorghum</u>

Millet and sorghum are staple food crops in Mali, grown on about 75 percent of land cultivated in cereals,[32] and — unlike corn and rice — are consumed on the whole width of the territory, with a very

---

[32] MSU 2011.

low gap between quantities consumed by city dwellers and rural dwellers.[33] They currently contribute to over 50 percent of total cereal production[34]. Given their relatively low cost for consumers compared to rice and their large share of domestic cereal production, millet and sorghum make a critical contribution to national food security, particularly that of rural farm households that are not well integrated into markets. Furthermore, being far more drought tolerant than rice or maize, millet and sorghum are often the only staple food crops that can be grown outside of irrigated areas. Most smallholder farmers grow millet and sorghum for household consumption, with only about 20 percent of the total production marketed[35]. Production is usually only sufficient to support the household for four to six months and must be supplemented with purchases from the market for the remainder of the year, creating a market opportunity for expanded production. Yields for both crops are low, often less than one metric ton per hectare, primarily grown on small plots of land averaging one hectare in total area. Sorghum and millet are generally grown in marginal and rain-fed areas, with little to no use of certified seeds, improved varieties, or chemical fertilizers, and primarily with manual or animal labor. Cowpea is frequently intercropped with sorghum and millet to enrich the soil, and provide an additional protein source for household consumption and fodder for livestock. Adopting a systems development approach will also positively affect corn grown in the Sikasso region, as the three crops are generally produced in the same areas and will benefit from improved storage and access to inputs, including fertilizer.

Figure 2. Millet & Sorghum Production Zones

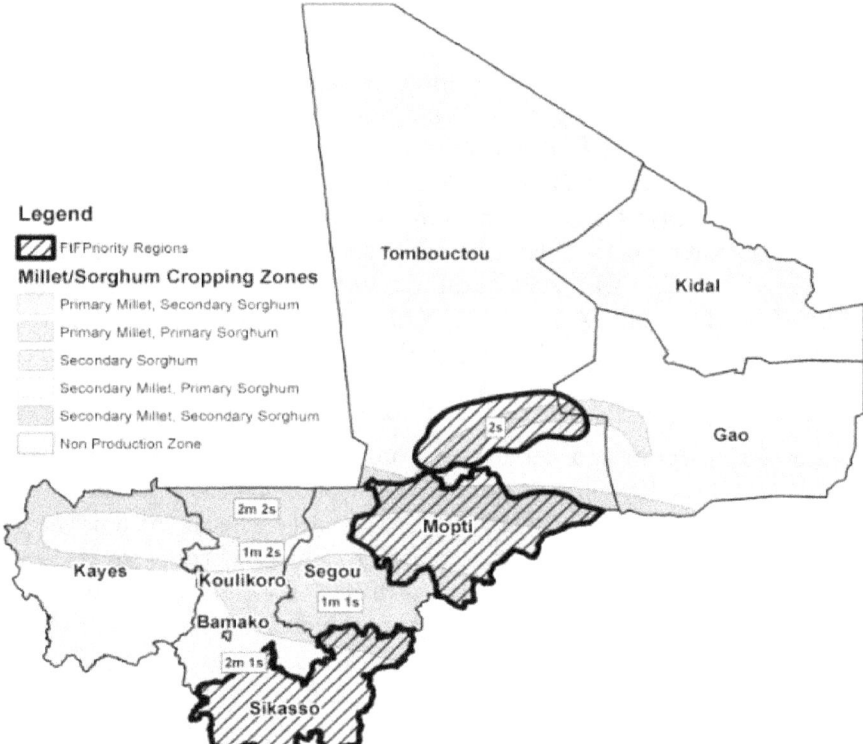

Production and yields for millet and sorghum have increased much more modestly than those for rice and maize; between 1990/91 and 2008/09, production increased by 68 percent for millet and 42 percent for sorghum, compared to 224 percent for maize and 228 percent for rice. Annual yield growth rates were 1.2 percent for millet and only 0.8 percent for sorghum, while area expansion averaged 2.1 percent for millet and 1.3 percent for sorghum. As the above evidence indicates, production increases of both grains were driven by farmers expanding the area of production instead of improving yields, a pattern that will likely be unsustainable in the future[36]. Newly developed planting methodologies, combined with improved seeds and the use of improved inputs can boost yields while catering to farmers' varying appetites for risk. It is estimated that

[33] PNIP-SA 2010.
[34] Ministry of Agriculture, January 2009.
[35] MSU, 2011.
[36] MSU 2011.

low-input solutions can produce a 20-30 percent increase in yields over farmers' conventional seeds with the farmer using the same techniques as before. High-input solutions require farmers to invest approximately $100/ha into chemical fertilizers and work best with animal traction, but can increase yields from 75 percent to 100 percent over current varieties grown with traditional levels of fertilizer[37]. Both systems work best with water conservation efforts and by adding organic fertilizers such as manure. Each of these potential interventions allows farmers to make their own choices about whether they make most sense for their individual farm, situation, budget, and risk profile[38].

Several USG/Mali-funded activities such as PMP, INTSORMIL (Sorghum and Millet Collaborative Research Support Program CRSP), and IICEM (Initiative Integrée de Croissance Economique au Mali) have made inroads in this area, but the data available on the total area of millet/sorghum planted to improved varieties and marketed through producer organizations is a very small share of the total area of millet and sorghum. The growth rate in terms of the expansion of areas planted with improved seeds has been remarkable. From 2009 to 2010 there was an increase from 685 ha to 4,340 ha. If this growth can be sustained for several years there could be a revolution in the production of millet and sorghum for commercial purposes. Developing intercropping opportunities with other products is another way for farmers to increase their income from millet and sorghum farming. Partnerships with private sector companies like SUDAGRI that intercrop *jatropha* as a natural wind break with millet and sorghum in the Sikasso region can benefit both farmers and the company.

In addition to the technical options for significantly increasing yields and production, there is a considerable need to develop better market output links between farmer cooperatives and processors who are willing to pay premium prices for regular supplies of higher quality millet and sorghum. High price volatility characterizes the millet and sorghum market. Prices usually crash at the immediate end of the growing season when farmers sell their crops *en masse* before they can spoil and then peak a few months before the beginning of the subsequent growing season when supplies are low. Improved storage facilities and a wider application of processing can even out prices by establishing a price floor and by creating demand for high-quality millet and sorghum. Prices can also be supported by developing markets for value-added processed goods such as nutritional supplements, bread, beer, and different packaging configurations. For this to happen, the quality of product that processors receive must be improved. The sorghum and millet processing market has many local processors that transform their products using unimproved raw materials and thus cannot receive a high price for their finished goods.

Large processors are more attentive to quality of the raw materials received, and often cannot receive a consistent supply of quality goods for their mills. Significant opportunities exist to boost prices at all stages of the value chain by encouraging the adoption of a uniform system of quality standards and grading, and by facilitating contracts between growers, aggregators, traders, and processors.

Both men and women are very active in production, processing, storage, and marketing activities along the millet and sorghum value chain. They are jointly active in land preparation, plowing, weeding, thinning, transport to market, marketing, and retailing. Men are more involved in preparing the land, weeding, thinning, seed treatment, applying fertilizer, cutting during the harvest, sacking, weighing, and aggregating stocks from multiple sellers. Women are more involved in sowing, gathering the harvest, winnowing, and preparation for home consumption. Notably, women are absent from significant marketing functions, including intermediary stages requiring mobility, handling cash transactions, and wholesaling. Significant constraints to greater women's participation in the millet and sorghum sector include domestic chores limiting the time that women have to engage in economic activities, limited

---

[37] MSU 2011.
[38] Foltz 2010.

access to credit, low-capacity female producer organizations, laws that limit women's ability to open separate businesses, cultural barriers that restrict the movement of women, an inability to own land, and the poor enforcement of laws that promote gender equality[39]. Clearly, any interventions under Feed the Future must take into account the constraints that women face in the context of maintaining social and familial stability and in keeping with cultural norms. Most significantly, increasing women's access to credit and to market information is critical to improve women's participation in marketing functions and to assist their family members in the decision-making process with the goal of gaining a greater share of value chain profits. Other opportunities include targeting women in capacity-building trainings to boost their productivity, and by improving the agricultural and commercial enabling environment through policy reforms that allow for greater gender equity in land titling and distribution.

<u>Rice Value Chain Analysis</u>

Increases in per capita rice consumption are mainly due to increased urbanization in large cities; however, about 90 percent of households in Mali consume rice[40]. National consumption of rice increased from 34 kg per person in 1989 to 53 kg per person in 1998 to an estimated 57 kg per person in 2007, [41] although import statistics suggest per capita consumption is even higher than the official consumption statistics. The recurrent drought that has disrupted the regular supply of millet and sorghum in recent years is also driving increases in rice consumption due to the stability of rice supplies through national production in irrigated areas and through imports. Mali currently produces about 85 percent of its rice consumed, with the remainder imported (278,000 tons in 2008/2009), representing $69.2 million in foreign expenditures in 2009[42].

The Office du Niger (ON) is the primary rice growing zone in Mali. It is characterized by large-scale investments in rice farming that allow farmers to enjoy the benefits of full water control, significantly higher yields, and high economic returns. The vast majority of smallholder farmers cannot afford the high up-front infrastructure costs, recurring maintenance costs, and high doses of fertilizer required to maintain production in that region, however, prompting policy makers and researchers to explore the potential for intensifying different production systems in other regions. These include irrigated village perimeters, controlled flooding zones, and lowland *bas fonds* areas as well as rain fed upland areas. Rice produced in the *bas fonds* and other areas tends to be cultivated for household use on smaller plots within the context of a more diversified cropping mix. The use of improved technologies in these areas is less widespread and yields under 1MT/ha are common. Significant opportunities to further diversify rice cropping systems in Mali also exist by encouraging simultaneous fish production in irrigated rice growing areas and by intensifying vegetable production during the off-season rotation. Both interventions have great potential to improve household nutrition as well as provide another source of income, particularly for women. The PNIP-SA outlines ambitious targets for investing and increasing production in each of these rice cropping systems with the aim of becoming self-sufficient in rice.

While issues of gender equity are generally similar to those as described in the millet and sorghum value chain, some significant differences are also present. Women generally perform the more labor-intensive aspects of rice production, including transplanting seedlings, and drying harvested rice stalks. Gender equity in the rice value chain is limited by men's control of key factors of production (i.e., land, inputs, and finance), and by the time constraints placed on women where they perform most household chores. As heads of the household, men make most marketing decisions in the rice value chain and control revenue. A major opportunity exists to achieve gender equity, however, by focusing on the Southern

---

[39] IICEM. IICEM Gender Analysis and Action Plan for the Millet-Sorghum Value Chain." 2011.
[40] USAID 2009.
[41] USDA 2009.
[42] INSAT, Comité de validation des statistiques du commerce extérieur du Mali.

rain fed zone around Sikasso where women predominantly cultivate and market rice grown in the *bas fonds*. Women account for around 47 percent of the total participation in the *bas fonds*, pointing the way toward achieving greater gender equity in this production zone and expanding the lessons learned there to other regions. Building capacity in women's farmer organizations is another way toward building gender equity. Development partners can work through these organizations to build the capacity of women to manage and warehouse receipt storage systems so they can better manage their rice crops and secure control of monetary assets.[43] Another significant opportunity for women potentially exists in the processing and sorting stages, which are currently handicapped by a lack of grades and standards and quality control. Development partners can support women-managed SME "mini-rice mills" and informal market retailers/sorters who hand-sort and clean mixed lots of rice. Partners could work to assist these businesses in capturing part of the 15 percent to 20 percent price premium for the high-end rice market segment[44].

Figure 3. Rice Production Zones

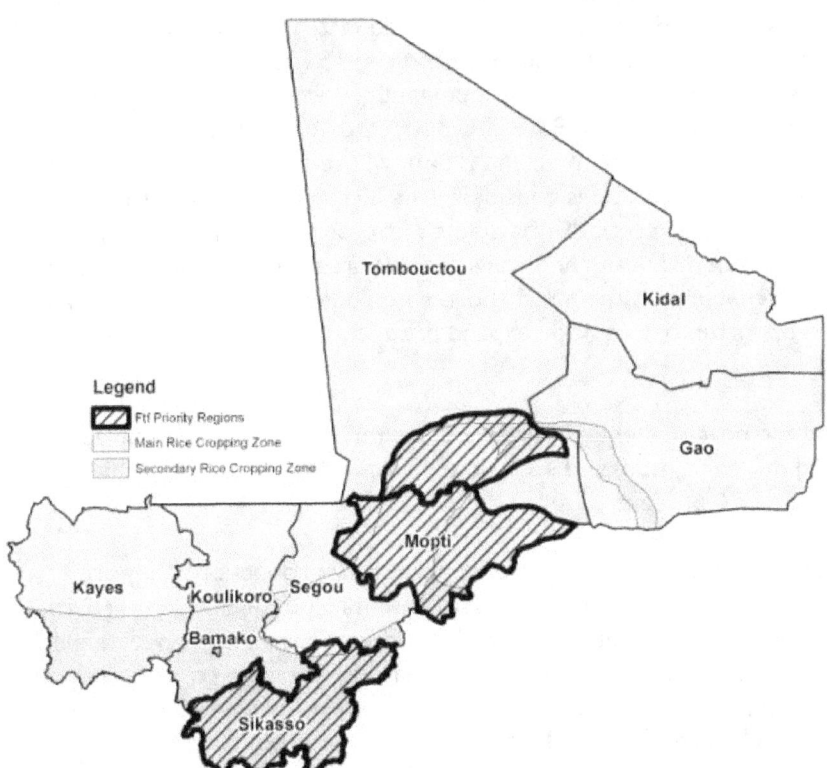

If Malian rice is to compete with imported rice, first in local urban markets and second in sub-regional urban markets, its quality, particularly in terms of cleanliness, must also improve along the value chain. Focusing on quality will allow rice to play a greater role in income generation and poverty reduction for rural farmers, especially women in the *bas fonds* areas. Small and medium entrepreneurs will have important roles to play in building processing capacity through small rice mills and by developing voluntary market standards. For example, the USG has already launched several such entrepreneurs through its earlier programs, the branded *Star of the Delta* rice producer. Linkages between millers, wholesalers, and rice producer organizations will also be important to support the construction of better storage facilities and to ensure clear market pathways for farmers associations adhering to improved quality standards. Improvements in productivity, storage, processing and quality standards will allow Mali to not only become self-sufficient in rice and to capture more added value, but also to supply exports to meet regional demand. Technical and market level intervention will need to be accompanied by a commitment by the GOM to improve the policy environment, particularly as it relates to subsidies, voluntary market standards, and import exonerations.

---

[43] Diarra, Salifou B. and Lenaghan, Tom. *Global Food Security Response – Mali Rice Study*. August 2009.
[44] Michigan State University, 2011.

Initial evidence suggests that, in the aggregate, household rice consumption in Mali is equal to more than double the amount of household income derived from rice production. Rice price increases, therefore, have a significant impact on the poverty rate, with a 25 percent increase in the price of rice leading to a 1.5 percent increase in the poverty rate, and it is safe to assume that rising prices in recent years have contributed to rising poverty levels[45]. Building improved storage facilities can have a positive effect on food security, as they allow households to store rice without spoiling for a longer period of time and in a variety of climactic conditions. Finally, intercropping can contribute to food security because families can gain a more secure source of a diverse array of nutritious foods at the household instead of paying an elevated price for these goods at the market.

Livestock – cattle, sheep and goats

Livestock represent Mali's third most important export commodity, after gold and cotton. According to the most recently available data from the FAO, livestock and livestock products accounted for 39 percent of the value of Mali's 20 most important agricultural commodities in terms of the value of production[46]. Mali's cattle population was approximately 8.8 million head in 2010, up from an estimated 5.2 million head in 1992. Mali also has an estimated 11.3 million sheep and 15.7 million goats[47]. Because of the importance of livestock to the Malian economy and its important growth potential, improving livestock value chains is one of the top priorities of the PNIP-SA. Both cattle and small ruminants are dominant in the northern regions of Gao, Kidal, Timbuktu, and Mopti, where these animals constitute a critical component of pastoral livelihoods. While beef is considered an "urban meat" and cattle are is exported in large quantities, small ruminants are typically the staple meat for poor, rural households in Mali, therefore interventions to improve animal health and weight in this area should improve access to this potentially important protein source. Further, the much shorter reproductive cycles of sheep and goats offer smallholder farmers the opportunity to quickly expand production when adequate feed resources are available[48].

Increasing livestock production and the development of dairy products through the value chain approach can reduce the import of powdered milk, and estimated 15 billion FCFA, and contribute to achieving the targeted agricultural GDP growth rate of 6 percent[49].

Women are very active in small ruminant production and also work in dairy production. They are actively involved in the marketing of locally produced dairy products as an income-generating activity. The introduction and adoption of low-cost technologies for products largely produced by women like animal feed and strengthening the capacity of women's cooperatives can reduce their cost of production and increase their income. For example, women are the primary sellers of natural supplemental feeds such as native grasses, legumes and shrubs in addition to by-products of crop products such as stovers, pod hulls, and leaves from crop plants such as peanuts. Women sell these items in livestock markets and women's groups participate in small ruminant fattening enterprises. Interventions that can assist women's groups and other producers to develop least cost feed rations and receive information on supplemental feed quality will optimize supplemental feeding practices for fattening and will reduce overfeeding. As with the millet and sorghum value chain, improved access to credit and market information is critical for women to assist their family members in the decision-making process and garner a greater share of the value of their livestock sold.

---

[45] Nouve, Kofi and Quentin Woods. "Impact of Rising Rice Prices and Policy Responses in Mali".
[46] FAO. 2008.
[47] MSU 2011.
[48] MSU 2011.
[49] PNIP-SA 2010.

Figure 3. Livestock Migration and Production Zones

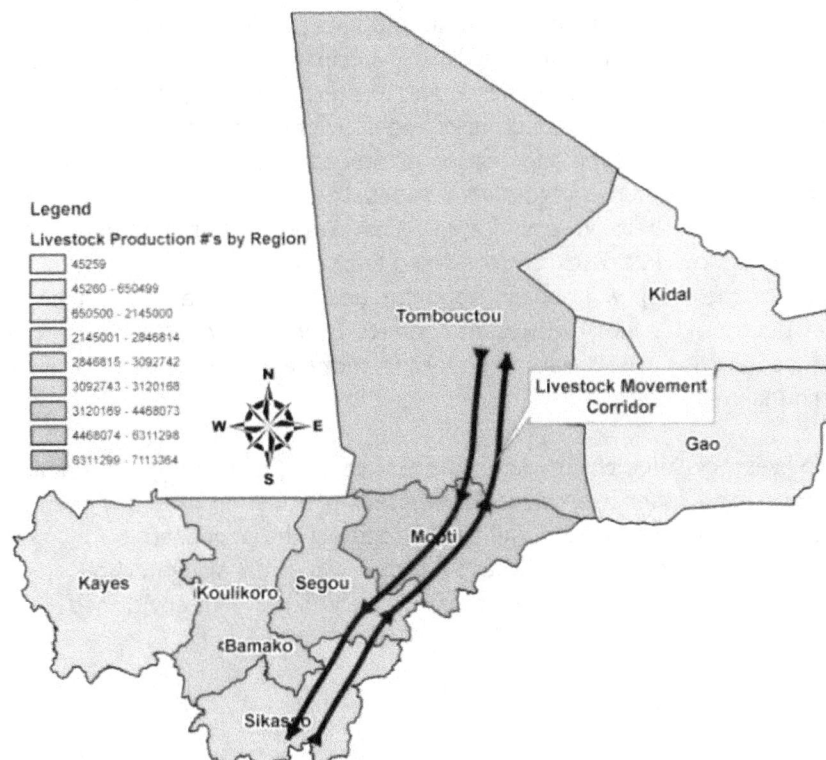

The major constraints facing the livestock sector include: 1) diminished animal health due to the reduction in forage supply and inadequate sources of nutrition during the dry season, 2) a general lack of marketing options for the majority of producers, 3) a lack of information and the capacity to diversify income streams through other enterprises such as livestock fattening, and 4) a lack of information to better manage risk.

Malian livestock primarily depend on forage found in natural pastures, which is in turn heavily dependent on the quantity of rain received during the rainy season from May to September. During the long dry season from October to April, both the quantity and quality of forage sharply declines, especially during periods of drought, which negatively affects animal health and weight. Priority interventions can address the primary constraint of forage quantity and quality in the pasturelands around water points because it directly affects animal health and the weight of the saleable animals. Limitations on the amount of forage available are also linked to a reduction in land area for rangeland forage production. The increased production of crops in the Niger River delta and the overuse of pasture lands have reduced grazing reserves that traditionally provided forage during the dry season. An opportunity exists to develop community-based rangeland rehabilitation programs to restore the pasture land reserves in these areas. This initiative can be integrated with better planning for cropland to ensure that adequate reserve areas remain to reduce conflict over grazing rights. Other important areas for investment in the livestock value chain are at water points along the migratory pathways and their associated pasture areas.

Community associations can be strengthened at existing and new watering areas to provide for better management and maintenance of water sources. User fees levied by the community associations provide income to support the intensified management of these areas. Communal land commissions can facilitate compacts and agreements between the community associations, migrant herders, and pastoralists while providing a framework to enforce the agreements.

A previous USG-funded livestock project, Mali Livestock II, and subsequent external donor-funded PRODESO and PADESO projects point toward ways in which the Malian livestock sector can be better developed, particularly by transforming the livestock sector from a traditional production model to one based on marketing and value-added approaches. At current off-take rates, the demand for livestock will likely grow faster than supply over the next 10 years, leading to higher prices and increased competition between the domestic and export markets for the available supply. Modest increases in off-take due to, for example, improved animal nutrition that allows animals to reach a marketable size earlier, could dramatically increase the marketed surplus. As a result, many opportunities for greater private sector involvement exist in the specific areas of water point management and fodder production. Private entrepreneurs can also expand their health services offerings, including vaccination, and thereby further improve production and marketable quality of livestock. Domestic and regional marketing systems can be strengthened where non-tariff trade barriers such as roadblocks and illicit charges add significant costs to Malian exporters. Greater dissemination of the information produced by the preexisting market information system will provide herders and women engaged in animal husbandry with better pricing and information about when and where to sell their livestock for the greatest profit. Research and extension on least-cost feed rations and on market research to expand exports to Mali's northern neighbors as well as to the Gulf (e.g., for the Hadj) will expand opportunities for effective interventions. Finally, the EU is financing the construction of a major highway to connect Timbuktu with the rest of the country. This road will allow farmers and other private sector players to more efficiently transport live animals to export points in southern Mali.

As a note, USG's investments in the livestock value chain will encompass cattle, sheep and goats. Poultry is a separate category and hides, hooves, and other byproducts of livestock production have not been considered. Live animals and household dairy consumption will be the focus of the proposed programming. Butchered meat was not considered due to issues with the cold chain, slaughterhouses, and the transportation infrastructure that would require much greater investments than envisioned under Feed the Future.

3.3   GEOGRAPHIC AND SECTOR FOCUS

Working with the Government of Mali and donor organizations, USG/Mali identified three geographic regions in which to focus its investments, based primarily on the criteria of agricultural production potential, nutritional indicators, and poverty, but also taking into account other factors, such as political considerations, population size, the presence of current USG/Mali programs, the presence and leverage potential of other donor programs, physical accessibility, and safety and security issues. An analysis of the eight regions of Mali based on the above criteria suggested that USG/Mali could have the most impact by concentrating on three regions: Sikasso, Mopti and Timbuktu. Additional activities can be planned in the MCC area of Segou region to help ensure sustainability of this USG investment.

Table 2 illustrates some of the indices used to select the three regions. The number of farms operating in key value chains was used as a proxy for agricultural potential, while the percentage of stunted and wasted children was used for nutritional status. Within Table 2 the poverty rate of all residents was measured as two standard deviations below the norm, as indicated in the 2006 Demographic and Health Survey (DHS).

Within these large and diverse regions, USG/Mali further identified specific areas where development clusters could leverage the abilities of multiple development partners to deliver the most efficient and effective impact in areas of greatest need. USG/Mali identified the zones of greatest agricultural potential in terms of irrigable hectares or heads of livestock and the specific communes that the GOM has targeted for agricultural development. Geographic Information System (GIS) tools were utilized to map the locations of various health, education, food assistance and nutrition programs to determine where immediate development partners operated in the focus regions, and then aligned these with communes of importance under the GOM's poverty reduction strategy (see Annex G-I for GIS maps). They were in turn overlaid with the zones having the poorest nutritional status as well as the locations of leading agricultural production basins close to major markets, water sources, and a transportation infrastructure. On the basis of these analyses, and consultations and discussions with the GOM and other development partners, USG/Mali was able to develop its sub-geographies and targets for the Feed the Future program.

As shown in Table 2, Sikasso is the most populous region of Mali . This region has some of the highest poverty rates and poorest nutritional indicators in the country, despite the fact that large quantities of millet, sorghum, corn, rice, and livestock are produced and processed in the area. Within Sikasso, USG/Mali will focus and concentrate its efforts in the administrative *cercles* of Koutiala and Yorosso for millet and sorghum, Bougouni for sorghum, Kadiolo for livestock, and in the Sikasso *cercle* in all three value chains.

Table 2. Regional Analysis

Region	% Total pop.	# farms in millet / sorghum	# farms in rice	# of cattle	% Poverty	% of stunting	% wasting
Sikasso	**18**	110	24	1085	83	**45**	16
Segou	17	138	24	768	71	40	15
Koulikoro	16	156	12	977	75	39	16
Kayes	14	88	7	728	50	31	15
Mopti	15	**158**	**43**	**1907**	**89**	41	13
Timbuktu	5	31	31	689	61	44	17
Gao / Kidal	4	21	29	635	23	~33	~20
Bamako	11	4	1	22	24	23	14

The Mopti region, located in the Sahel belt, is the most significant livestock production region with large amounts of forage produced near the intersection of the Niger and Bani rivers. Mopti has the highest rates of poverty and some of the worst nutritional indicators in Mali. Within Mopti, USG/Mali will focus its interventions in the Bankass and Koro *cercles* (comprising the Seno production basin) for millet and rice; Djenne, Mopti, and Tenenkou for rice; and in Tenenkou and Mopti for livestock.

Timbuktu is the northernmost region of Mali and its inclusion in the Feed the Future strategy is essential to support the general stability and comprehensive development of Mali as a whole. FTF investments can reduce perceived disparities by integrating residents of northern areas into southern ones through trade and investment linkages. Residents of this area produce significant quantities of livestock and rice due to the presence of inland lakes. Increased production and sales of these agricultural products can alleviate food insecurity and generate income in the north. Herders will be able to more efficiently migrate their animals to the South through the development of water access points and improved pasture lands. Capacity-building investments in water management associations can encourage youth to enter the agriculture sector and increase its productivity. Timbuktu also has some of the worst rates of stunting and wasting in Mali, even though this region has a lower population than others. Within Timbuktu, USG/Mali will concentrate its efforts in the Goundam, Nianfunke, and Timbuktu *cercles* in rice and livestock, and Dire in rice, to build on current Food for Peace investments.

USG/Mali will also include the two communes in the Alatona area of the Segou region in its FTF strategy, also supported by the Mission's education, health and local governance activity programs. This area is the focus of a major MCC investment in rice production that is irrigating 5,000 hectares out of a 22,000 hectare zone. Around 70 percent of the population has virtually no education and the region is among the poorest in Mali. USG/Mali will not focus on rice production in this area, but instead will focus on building institutional sustainability among water management boards and producer organizations, and on rice marketing activities. USG/Mali will also learn from MCC's previous work in land titling and land administration systems in its communities outside of the Alatona area.

4. FEED THE FUTURE PROGRAM OBJECTIVES, STRUCTURE, AND IMPLEMENTATION

4.1 FEED THE FUTURE IMPLEMENTATION UNDER USAID FORWARD

Feed the Future in Mali will be implemented under the principles of USAID Forward by a variety of partners in the GOM, the donor and NGO community, the private sector, universities and the whole of U.S. Government. USG/Mali plans to continue supporting some existing programs with activities in nutrition and value chain development. These will be reviewed and work plans will be adjusted to bring projects in line with our Feed the Future strategy and target geographies. Much of the implementation, however, will be conducted through new projects to be developed in the next year with the explicit objectives of including new and non-traditional partners, of doing smaller direct awards and of working through government and other local structures as much as possible. USG/Mali has grouped FTF activities in agriculture and nutrition into the program areas listed below. Some of these will be new procurements or continuing programs and others will be accomplished through leveraging resources and expertise from other USG or donor partners. Monitoring and evaluation activities will comprise around 10 percent of the total budget and will be conducted at the project level. Gender analyses and environmental reviews will be considered and integrated into project management and monitoring plans.

USG/Mali will continue to provide institutional support for local capacity-building through the CPS and has recently conducted a domestic resource cost analysis to better align the PNIP-SA with the CAADP recommendations. As development of the PNISA continues, USG/Mali will support the GOM's CAADP alignment with additional technical analyses while coordinating its work through the sector-wide approach, the *Plan du passage a l'approche sectorial*. In turn, the GOM is supporting the USG/Mali FTF strategy by allocating three full-time employees with the Ministry of Agriculture to coordinate GOM and USG/Mali PNISA and FTF interventions, and their strategic alignment. Additionally, the GOM is financing 15 percent of the PNIP-SA and has called on the private sector to finance 20 percent of its interventions. The Government of Mali has asked the donor community to finance the remaining 65 percent.

See Table 3 for an intervention summary and Annex F for a more detailed discussion of specific and targeted interventions for the Feed the Future program.

Technological Advancement

Education and Training

University Capacity-Building: USG/Mali will provide direct grants to educational institutions such as the University of Bamako / IPR to build on their core strengths and improve agricultural and nutrition education at multiple levels. Activities under the extension services program area will be linked to higher education and research institutions to ensure that all training is of a high technical caliber and reflects best practices needed for young generations to engage in transformational functions. USG/Mali will continue to support several agricultural research partnerships with U.S. universities and international research centers that will provide opportunities to train Master's and Ph.D. level students. Women will be particularly targeted in recruitment for these programs, as they are currently underrepresented as educators and researchers at the higher levels. USG/Mali can also potentially partner with programs like the USDA-funded International Science and Education competitive grants program to improve the quality of instruction, training, and extension services available to farmers by strengthening the educational curriculums of top national institutions.

Table 3. Intervention Summary

Intervention Programs	Intervention Activities
Community Level Capacity Building	• Develop business and organizational management skills of agricultural cooperatives, organizations • Technical assistance to communities for management of infrastructures and natural resources, and to leverage resources for their farming community • Increase both individual's and communities' knowledge and awareness of factors contributing to malnutrition and poor health status • Strengthen communities' capacity to prevent and manage malnutrition and govern health resources and facilities • Strengthen land commissions to demarcate land under customary law • Ensure sustainability of MCC investments by building capacity of land management organizations and water management boards in Alatona region.
Improved Seed Sector	• Build research/adaptation and extension capacity of IER • Develop businesses and technical capacities of community seed producers • Build business and marketing capacities of seed distributers • Develop private commercial seed business including the IPR/Katibougou seed lab
Small Infrastructure Development	• Storage facilities (millet/sorghum, rice) • Water management structures and small-scale irrigation systems (rice) • Water points and pastureland development (livestock) • Multiple-use water access points to improve household access to water
Millers, Processors, Traders and Marketing	• Improve access to technology; product development • Facilitate contracts with farmers • Develop system of uniform grades and standards • Improve marketing of products, including complementary and fortified foods
Credit and Finance	• Capacity-building of all actors to improve their banking and credit management capacities • Work with existing financial institutions to establish credit guarantees for agricultural loans and technical assistance in assessing credit risk • Scale-up warehouse receipt systems and develop savings schemes among farmer's groups • Integrate delivery of health education and behavior change messages into credit service platforms

Enabling Policy Environment for Agriculture and Nutrition	• Advocate for policy changes crucial to enabling the agriculture and business, including removal of trade barriers; fertilizer and seed policy; interest rate subsidies; land policy; the legal framework; contract enforcement; biosafety and phytosanitary standards; regional trade corridors; intellectual property rights regimes; and reforms in the commerce, tax, and customs offices • Build off of MCC investments in land titling in the Alatona area to strengthen land administration capabilities of targeted communes in Sikasso, Mopti, and Timbuktu. • Work with other donors and partners to support an elevated inter-sectoral nutrition office in the GOM that can effectively promote and coordinate nutrition policy • Through the Scaling-Up Nutrition (SUN) process, continue to support the GOM as needed in collaboration with other donors • Continue to provide technical support to the Ministry of Health to reevaluate ten-year health strategy and to plan for the next ten years with stronger emphasis on role of nutrition in health • Support the GOM to enact and enforce industrial food-based fortification legislation
Health System Capacity Building (GHI)	• Continue to support strengthening of service delivery of maternal, child and reproductive health services, including nutrition services such as vitamin A, deworming, mass treatment for NTDs, iron/folate supplementation, and CMAM • Continue to invest heavily in strengthening malaria prevention, control and treatment (Presidential Malaria Initiative) • Provide technical assistance to strengthen and support the health information management system in Mali as well as logistics management systems
Agricultural Research	• Strengthen research institutions, such as IER, National Health Laboratory, and IPR • Continue research partnerships, such as those with the Livestock CRSP and ICRISAT • Improve crops and livestock genetic material
Nutrition Research	• Operational research to determine effective interventions to improve anemia prevention and treatment efforts at the community level • Improve the service delivery of CMAM through a facility-to-facility quality improvement approach • Through research partnerships, develop recipes for household and small-scale production of complementary foods, to be disseminated via agricultural and health platforms
Agricultural Extension and Advisory Services	• Strengthen government extension services to disseminate information on least cost animal rations, best agricultural practices, storage techniques, soil and water management, IPM, intercropping and other agronomic techniques • Develop programs to engage the private agribusiness sector • Agricultural and nutrition education activities through the University of Bamako/IPR • Support specialized agriculture training schools
SBCC and Social Marketing Program	• Launch an SBCC (Social Behavioral Change Communication)/Social Marketing program that will encompass all of the Social Marketing Behavior Change Communication (SBCC) under the Global Health Initiative (GHI) and FTF
Monitoring & Evaluation Systems	• Invest, along with the World Bank, in the Living Standards Measurement Survey (LSMS-ISA) • Support the Demographic and Health Survey, oversample in FTF intervention zones to establish baseline • Supporting a pilot program to create a cell phone-based method of collecting and sharing critical information, including market information

Geographic Area: All intervention programs will operate in all four geographical areas (Sikasso, Mote, Timbuktu, and two communes of Segou), with the qualification that Segou activities will not include livestock or millet/sorghum, and Timbuktu activities will exclude millet/sorghum.

Research & Dissemination

Agricultural Extension and Advisory Services: A BFS-managed program, *Modernizing Extension and Advisory Services,* will be engaged to design targeted activities to strengthen government extension services and to help launch pilot programs to engage the private agribusiness sector in this role. USG will build off investments in private enterprises by AGRA and other donors. Agricultural education activities through the University of Bamako / IPR and specialized agriculture training schools will further strengthen this program area. To address inequalities and reduce women's time-burden in the production and processing of millet and sorghum, USG will intentionally include women in the delivery of intensive farming techniques, and will improve women's access to more efficient inputs and processing technologies. Women will also be targeted for recruitment as agricultural extension agents; recent assessments of GOM extension services show that they are underrepresented in this discipline.

Improved Seed Sector: A reliable source of high-yield, quality seeds adapted to local conditions in Mali is essential to improve productivity and value-added processing. The development of and access to improved inputs will be addressed at the community level and through policy change; however, the foundational elements of seed production and distribution need to be strengthened. This will likely require a dedicated program to build the capacity of IER, seed dealers, and community seed production groups to improve the production and supply of certified seeds. These activities will also complement the work of WASA and ICRISAT to further strengthen the seed sector.

Agricultural Research: Strengthening research institutions such as IER, Laboratoire Central Vétérinaire, and the National Health Laboratory will go hand in hand with ensuring that global research innovations are adapted to meet farmers' needs. Existing research partnerships will be strengthened. Additional linkages to the Consultative Group on International Agricultural Research (CGIAR), especially IFPRI, International Livestock Research Institute (ILRI), and AfricaRice; and to U.S. universities and private R&D firms will continue to strengthen research capacity in Mali and ensure a pipeline of research innovations necessary for agricultural growth and improved nutrition. Finally, research conducted on key agricultural commodities like millet, sorghum, and rice will have spillover effects on cotton research, which is grown in the same area as these other crops.

Value Chain Development

Markets and Trade Development

Millers, Processors, Traders and Marketing: This program area will strengthen community-level capacity-building to connect farmers to aggregators, millers and processors in order to enhance supply and demand in these value chains. It may require a dedicated program to work specifically with millers and other processors to build technical expertise, enter into contracts with growers, access credit, develop a system of uniform grades and standards, and develop and market new products. It also links to the development of extension services, as extension agents can serve as an additional source of technical assistance for farmers, helping them ensure a higher quality, more abundant and more stable supply of raw materials. USG/Mali will deepen and strengthen its partnership with OMA to improve market information systems for cereals and livestock, including SMS updates provided via cellular telephone. Women can particularly benefit from improved livestock market information systems due to their significant role in *bas fonds* rice and small ruminant production and marketing. Additionally, USG/Mali is exploring partnership possibilities with major players in several agro-industries that would also contribute resources, expertise, and opportunities to this program.

Fostering Young Entrepreneurs: USG/Mali will work with the Education team on an out-of-school youth program that will work in partnership with the Ministry of Employment, the Ministry of Education and the Ministry of Agriculture, as well as private sector and civil society organization (e.g., youth organizations) to provide up to 10,000 youth with non-formal education, technical and vocational competencies, entrepreneurship skills and accompaniment support during transition from training to economic independence. Significant thematic linkages will be formed between the out-of-school youth program with value chain interventions to spur agricultural production, processing, and marketing.

Community Level Capacity Building: Many of the USG/Mali FTF interventions will be targeted at the community or producer organization level. Building capacity at this level to manage communal resources, access credit, develop business and organizational management skills, evaluate and adopt new technologies, administer land and resolve conflict, and negotiate contracts will be incorporated into the proposed range of interventions. USG/Mali will also target women's associations with access-to-credit and capacity development interventions while being sensitive and responsive to the unique challenges posed to the development of women's associations such as very low literacy rates, weak participation, women's time limitations, and gender perceptions. USG/Mali may implement a competitive small grants program to help implement commune-level development plans supportive of FTF. USG/Mali will also work with MCC in the Alatona area to build capacity among water management boards and in land management organizations in order to ensure sustainability of MCC investments in this area.

Infrastructure

Small Infrastructure Development: USG/Mali has already obtained technical feasibility studies for the planned structural investments in storage facilities, small-scale irrigation and water retention structures, and water points for livestock. An existing program will continue some construction activities. USG/Mali is currently negotiating a collaboration with German aid agencies GIZ and *Kreditanstalt für Wiederaufbau* (KFW) which implement a GOM program that could reduce start-up time and take advantage of economies of scale. Remote sensing capabilities employed by the U.S. Geological Survey (USGS) will identify water point sites to develop.

Credit & Finance

Access to Credit and Finance: USG/Mali will address this crucially important area through several entry points. Capacity-building work at the community level and at the miller/processor level will include training on business management, developing credit dossiers, and adult literacy and numeracy. USG/Mali will work directly with larger banks to establish a credit guarantee for agricultural loans and provide technical training to help them assess credit risk. An assessment team from the USAID Economic Growth, Agriculture, and Trade (EGAT) bureau and Development Credit Alliance (DCA) will investigate opportunities to work with regional economic players, such as the West Africa Economic and Monetary Union (WAEMU) and the Economic Community of West African States (ECOWAS), and to develop sources of medium-term agricultural credit.

Enabling Environment

Policy / Enabling Environment

Enabling Policy Environment for Agriculture and Nutrition: USG agencies, and the PTF will engage directly with the GOM to advocate for necessary policy changes to promote agriculture growth and better nutrition, and will commission analytical studies to inform policy dialogues. The top policy priority for the USG/Mali FTF strategy is to promote nutrition as an elevated cross-cutting issue in GOM ministries. This is followed by improving seed sector policy and intellectual property rights, weakening barriers to trade, land administration reform, and reforming fertilizer policy. A MicroCLIR study currently underway will point to specific areas of intervention where Feed the Future can make immediate, sustainable impacts in the enabling environment.

Major national strategies around health, social development, and nutrition are currently being developed, supported by USG/Mali through implementing partners, including ATN+ and MEASURE Evaluation. Helen Keller International supports wheat flour fortification in wheat mills and the development of legislation mandating wheat fortification in Mali. USG /Mali also provides central funding to UNICEF to address iodine deficiency, with is largely an issue of enforcing regulations that mandates that salt be fortified with iodine. Some policy changes, such as seed laws, plant variety protection, intellectual property rights enforcement and biosafety policy will require longer-term technical assistance. This may need a dedicated program to work with government partners and stakeholders in civil society and the private sector to enact functional and sustainable policy change.

Within the USG /Mali Mission, FTF will leverage the ability of the Governance and Communication team to build capacity in local commune governments, in line with the continuing GOM policy of devolving power to local governments. Outside of the Mission, USG /Mali will leverage its work with the CLDP in the field of intellectual property rights protection, and will work with the Department of State, the PTF, and USG/WA on seed policy and biosafety regulations, and trade barriers. A collaboration with the EU will build capacity in the agricultural CPS, and a partnership with KFW and GIZ will build capacity in the Ministry of Agriculture and in communal governments to better manage small infrastructure projects, including irrigation structures and water points. USG /Mali will also work with MCC to enact local-level policy reforms in water management and in land administration in targeted communes. MCC work in land titling will serve as a blueprint for USG /Mali investments to build capacity and strengthen land administration policy in targeted communes outside of the Alatona area.

Monitoring and Evaluation Systems Development and Strengthening

Dedicated Monitoring and Evaluation Systems: USG/Mali will invest, along with the World Bank, in the Living Standards Measurement Survey (LSMS-ISA) in order to furnish accurate local-level information to both national and local policy-makers. This tool will allow commune and other regional government bodies to more fully understand the socioeconomic situation in their localities and create policies that directly address their local context.

Nutrition

Nutrition System Strengthening

Health System Capacity Building: The USG /Mali Health team will use two existing bilaterals to improve service delivery of maternal and child health as well as reproductive health services, including nutrition services such as vitamin A, deworming, mass treatment for NTDs, iron/folate supplementation, and CMAM. These bilaterals have a mandate to strengthen health services from the national to the community level, and to support policy work around these issues. During the design phase, USG/Mali will determine whether health education training and the delivery of technical assistance will be conducted by the same implementer or by a parallel implementer that provides agriculture capacity-building services.

Social and Behavior Change Communication and Social Marketing Program: USG/Mali has developed a new 5-year SBCC/Social Marketing program that will encompass all SBCC under GHI and FTF. This program will include a subject matter expert for the entire portfolio of partners to develop messages and materials based on formative research that they would then tailor to the specific platform and audience of the project. This wheel and spoke approach of technical assistance will assure a level of quality control and harmony across platforms.

Nutrition Research: USG /Mali will buy into the Health Care Improvement Project, a central mechanism, to initiate new health care collaborative where health clinic personnel are brought together to analyze their service records and other available data in order to identify weaknesses and differences in approach. Following that step, clinic personnel then identify solutions based on what other clinics are reporting and use these results to improve their own service delivery. Additional funding will be used to address learning agenda priorities under GHI and other operational research to be identified during implementation.

Nutrition Monitoring and Evaluation: The USG /Mali Health team will allocate a portion of its budget to monitor and evaluate nutrition interventions over the five-year Feed the Future initiative.

4.2   FEED THE FUTURE RESULTS FRAMEWORK AND DEVELOPMENT HYPOTHESIS

The USG/Mali Feed the Future strategic goal is to increase agricultural production, improve nutritional statuses, especially of women and children, and reduce rural poverty among target beneficiaries (see Results Framework in Annex D). This goal relies on two main objectives each having the following development hypotheses, indicators and targets:

1. **Key Objective A**: Increase agricultural sector growth

Development Hypothesis: Through the investments outlined in this multi-year strategy, USG/Mali can achieve: 1) increases in agricultural production, 2) increases in producers' incomes, 3) improvements in nutritional status, and 4) a reduction in rural poverty among target beneficiaries by implementing the following:

- Improving, diversifying, and intensifying sustainable agriculture;
- Improving natural resources management;
- Developing and strengthening access to inputs, information, and credit to support the selected value chains;
- Building and improving agricultural production and storage-related infrastructures,
- Strengthening markets, including increased regional and international trade;
- Diversifying food production and consumption;
- Improving consumption and other nutrition-related behaviors; and
- Building and improving public-private partnerships

Risks:
- Climate change may adversely affect productivity increase in target area
- Locust and other pests infestation can devastate production
- Seasonal and input price fluctuation may affect incomes
- Poor policy affect enabling environment and limit investment in the agriculture sector
- Resources allocated to FTF are lower than expected
- Other donors reduce support to the agriculture sector
- Sustainability of natural resource management decisions
- Political instability

Assumptions:
- Rainfall remains within the normal range
- FTF resources will be leveraged with other donors
- GOM is committed to policy reforms
- Private sector is supportive to FTF programs
- Consistent level of funding by US government and other donors
- Financial institutions participate

Indicators for Objective A:

- Percent growth in agricultural GDP
- Expenditures of rural households (proxy for income)
- Gender perceptions index

2. **Key Objective B**: Improve nutritional status especially of women and children

Development Hypothesis: The poor nutritional status of women and children in Mali is a result of the interaction of complex cultural and socio-economic factors, and requires a multi-dimensional approach. Therefore, a context-specific, comprehensive package of health interventions focused on improving nutrition and hygiene related knowledge and behaviors, the access to and utilization of health services, clean water, and a more equitable distribution of monetary and non-monetary resources within the household will have a more significant impact on nutrition outcomes than agriculture production and income generation alone. Given the complex nature of the problem, the most effective response will be one that capitalizes on all available opportunities to reach the population, and as such would employ both traditional and non-traditional platforms for delivery.

Risks:
- Cultural gender inequities cannot be addressed in such a short time frame, and as such increases in productivity and income do not result in increased access to resources by women and children
- Communities require infrastructure improvements to improve behaviors that are outside of the budget
- Major reforms in health care financing are implemented mid-initiative that change the nature of the problem
- Resources allocated to FTF are lower than expected
- Agricultural beneficiaries are different from nutrition beneficiaries, resulting in a situation where only some receive the full package of interventions
- Other donors discontinue funding of major initiatives like CMAM and USG must divert resources to cover the efforts

Assumptions:
- Rainfall remains consistent with seasonal norms
- Political dynamics in neighboring countries do not destabilize Malian communities
- Existing health clinics are capable of meeting demand if it increases
- Commodities will be accessible by health clinics to treat cases
- Foods exist within the community to obtain a complete diet
- Drinking water is available in the community and can be made potable within the household
- Feed the Future intervention areas will overlap with existing GHI areas so to maximize the synergy between food availability, utilization and high quality health care to address nutrition.

Indicators for Objective B

- Prevalence of stunted children under five years of age
- Prevalence of wasted children under five years of age
- Prevalence of underweight women
- Prevalence of anemia among women of reproductive age
- Prevalence of anemia among children 6-59 months
- Prevalence of exclusive breastfeeding children < 6 months
- Prevalence of children 6-23 months with minimum acceptable diet
- Prevalence of households with moderate or severe hunger (Household Hunger Scale)
- Women's Dietary Diversity Score

The following two indicators will also be included in the FTF results framework, but baseline data is unavailable at this time:

- Prevalence of households with moderate or severe hunger (Household Hunger Scale)
- Women's Dietary Diversity: Mean number of food groups consumed by women of reproductive age

4.3   INTERMEDIATE RESULTS

4.3.1   Key Objective A: Increase Agricultural Sector Growth

Intermediate Result A.1: Improved Agricultural Productivity

Through this intermediate result, USG/Mali will increase both agricultural and livestock productivity and will promote the production of nutritious food in sufficient quantities and in a sustainable manner to achieve food security and reduce poverty in the targeted regions. Management practices will be introduced in such a way that productivity increases do not place unsustainable demands on scarce resources such as water. System resilience will be enhanced through better management as well, thereby helping farmers to adapt to climate change. To complement these investments, USG/Mali will build institutional capacity in the public sector in the key areas of improving the efficiency of government planning, implementation, and oversight processes. The research sector will be strengthened to ensure a pipeline of technologies relevant to producers in Mali. Intermediate result A.1 will be achieved through the following sub-intermediate results:

1. Enhanced human and institutional capacity development for increased agricultural sector productivity.

2. Enhanced technology development, dissemination, management and innovation.

3. Improved agricultural policy environment to increase productivity.

4. Agricultural producer organizations strengthened.

5. Negative impacts of global climate change mitigated.

The impact of the projected increases in agricultural productivity can be expressed through the gross margins of targeted commodities, which in turn will result in the improvement of other areas.

Intermediate Result A.2: Expanding markets and trade

Past experiences have shown that food security cannot be attained in a sustainable manner without giving market incentives to producers. Emphasizing production increases without investing in processing, marketing, and other steps of the value chain ensures that any gains will be ephemeral. Therefore, USG/Mali will work to expand internal and external markets and trade. Intermediate result A.2 will be achieved through the following sub-intermediate results:

- Enhanced human and institutional capacity development for agribusiness growth
- Enhanced agricultural trade
- Property rights to land and other productive assets strengthened
- Improved post-harvest market information systems
- Improved access to business development and sustainable risk management

Although there is no target available at this time, the value of intra-regional exports of targeted agricultural commodities (e.g., millet, sorghum, rice, and livestock) and their domestic trade value is expected to increase.

Intermediate Result A.3: Increased private sector investment in agriculture and nutrition related activities

The GOM's agricultural policies cannot be effective without support from the private sector. Its involvement will be essential to broaden access to credit among all agricultural value chain actors, especially in the critical areas of agricultural inputs and processing equipment; provide extension services to producer organizations; facilitate contracts between producers and processors of agricultural commodities; and improve market information systems. USG/Mali will work to strengthen the ability of the private sector to assume a larger role in the agricultural sector and to increase investment in activities that contribute to agricultural growth and improved nutrition. No sub-intermediate result is planned under this IR.

4.3.2 Key Objective B: Improve Nutritional Status, Especially of Women and Children

As nutrition is an investment area under both Feed the Future and the Global Health Initiative, the intermediate results and indicators will be tracked and reported through both initiatives.

Intermediate Result B.1: Increased resilience of vulnerable communities and households

Activities under this IR include increasing food security by improving production and productivity in targeted vulnerable communities, and by developing mechanisms and support systems to reinforce the capacity of these populations to withstand periodic shocks. The capacity of community disaster preparedness committees to regularly collect early warning data is being developed. The information collected will feed into the national famine early warning system. Early warning and "surge" capacity components allow partners to respond to emergency needs in the event of slow and rapid onset disasters. The agricultural production of poor farmers will be increased with greater access to improved inputs, higher yielding seeds, and irrigation.

Organizational support for cooperative activities to add value to products and get them to both local and export markets will bolster community and household resilience. Food aid will have an immediate impact in terms of protecting lives and maintaining consumption levels while also contributing to longer term impacts. It will thus enhance community and household resilience to shocks, helping people build more durable and diverse livelihood bases through increased assets and resources, and strengthening individual capabilities through improvements in health, nutrition and education. This approach means that food aid-supported activities will constitute a means to reduce vulnerability.

Intermediate result B.1 will be achieved through the following sub-intermediate results:

- The capacity of communities to manage risks and cope with shocks resulting from vulnerability is strengthened
- Livelihood strategies are more profitable and resilient

Intermediate Result B.2: Improved access to diverse and quality foods

An important goal of the USG/Mali Feed the Future program is to improve access of a diverse array of nutritious foods to reproductive age women and children less than 2 years old. The program will encourage farmers to produce nutritious crops and foods such as cowpea, horticulture products, and fish through intercropping within the production system of priority value chains. The program will also encourage women and children to consume more dairy products; this will be achieved by improving the health of livestock. To this end, USG/Mali will work with IER and IPR to introduce, produce, and disseminate millet and sorghum seeds biofortified with iron and zinc. In addition to this effort, the program will leverage the private sector to expand the access to and use of fortified supplemental nutritious additives while developing and marketing other fortified and ready-to-eat foods for children between six and 23 months old. This may also include the development of recipes that can be produced using local ingredients at the household level. Targets for this IR will include producers, mothers, child caretakers, and community health workers in the geographic focus areas. The strategy will be strengthened by encouraging policy reforms to support industrial food-based fortification legislation.

Intermediate result B.2 will be achieved through the following sub-intermediate results:

- Farmers have adopted improved post-harvest processing and storage techniques to maintain food quality and reduce post-harvest losses
- Farmers have adopted improved intercropping techniques to diversify foods available for consumption
- Dietary diversity for women and children under five is improved

Intermediate Result B.3: Improved nutrition related behaviors

USG/Mali will develop a new social and behavior change program that will deliver messages to improve care practices, health seeking behaviors, dietary diversity and hygiene practices. The program will build off of existing USG/Mali programs in various sectors through both traditional and non-traditional (e.g., agriculture extension workers, savings and loan groups, producer organizations, etc.) platforms to deliver key messages on nutrition. Based off of experience gained from both USG programs such as the Title II MYAP programs as well as other donor funded programs this program will use experience in Mali and the region in the design of approaches for SBCC work in target areas. Complementing this SBCC package will be the expansion of ORS/Zinc and point-of use water treatment nationwide in the private sector for treatment of diarrhea and water purity respectively. Intermediate result B.3 will be achieved through the following sub-intermediate results:

- Households have adopted improved dietary and care practices
- Households have adopted improved key hygiene behaviors

<u>Intermediate Result B.4: Increased Utilization of High Impact Services and Healthy Behaviors</u>

USG/Mali nutrition interventions will leverage the work of existing and new health programs that are working to strengthen the Malian health system at all levels including the facility, as well as the community through technical assistance and support to the Ministry of Health, community mobilization, and governance strengthening. With a focus on reducing maternal and child morbidity and mortality, current health programs focus on a package of high- impact, evidence-based interventions currently delivered through the existing programs (see Annex E) and will contribute to both FTF and GHI outcomes. USG /Mali Feed the Future nutrition interventions will include reinforcing and supporting existing micronutrient supplementation programs (e.g., vitamin A, deworming, NTD mass treatment, Fe/folate) and strengthening related preventative and curative care at the Centre de Santé Communautaire (CSCOM) level through vaccination, family planning, prenatal care, healthy baby visits and maternity services.

A major focus of FTF nutrition activities will be to determine constraints to adherence to the national protocol for the CMAM, and to work with facilities within the FTF areas to strengthen the service delivery, coverage, and cure rates for acute malnutrition. The majority of activities for these interventions will be delivered through the Ministry of Health facilities and community based health programs. Social and behavior change programming described above will raise awareness on the importance of health services to prevent illness and seek support for prevention and treatment of undernutrition. Women of reproductive age, children under five years old, and their families will be the primary target groups for these interventions. Intermediate result B.4 will be achieved through the following sub-intermediate result:

- Access, quality, and use of nutrition promotion and treatment services improved.

5. MONITORING AND EVALUATION

The USG/Mali FTF monitoring and evaluation approach will verify the development hypotheses outlined in the previous section by measuring the anticipated results and outcomes. This will be further elaborated in the Performance Management Plan (PMP) that will contain a final Results Framework developed by the Mission. The Mission retains the required FTF indicators, has omitted irrelevant performance indicators, and has added some key custom indicators. Much of the indicator data at the intermediate results level will be collected under the current projects. To ensure high quality data, particularly at the goal and objectives levels on agricultural sector growth, the national data collection unit will be reinforced.

<u>Performance Monitoring</u>

Activities monitoring will be carried out by the USG/Mali AEG and Health technical teams in collaboration with implementing partners (IP), other donors and the GOM. Each IP will develop a PMP to be reviewed and approved by the Mission. The PMP will include indicator reference sheets that will clearly explain indicator definitions, data collection methods, data limitations, baselines, targets, and other important elements. IPs will be responsible for collecting data and report on a regular basis. USG/Mali will conduct rigorous periodic field visits to monitor activities implementation and to perform Data Quality Assessments over the life of the programs. At the national and sub-national level, data will be obtained through assessments conducted by specialized private and/or national statistical data collection units in the health and agricultural sectors.

A solid performance review system will be developed and implemented to strategically analyze data and results to continuously inform and improve programs. The current Mission's semi-annual Portfolio Implementation Reviews (PIRs) process will be revised and strengthened to include IPs, other donors, the GOM and other USG agencies representatives.

The USG/Mali GIS unit will be used to not only constitute a central repository of performance data but to also perform spatial data analysis for better results monitoring and impact assessments. The Program Office has already established a collaboration path with USAID/Washington's bureau of Policy Planning and Learning (PPL) for that purpose.

The following indicators have already been identified at the goal-level and second-level objectives: Goal –level Indicators to monitor changes in the country context:

- Prevalence of Poverty: Percent of people living on less than $1.25/day
- Prevalence of underweight children under 5

Key objectives indicators:
- Percent growth in agricultural GDP
- Expenditures of rural households, as a proxy for income
- Gender perceptions index
- Prevalence of stunted children under 5
- Prevalence of wasted children under 5
- Prevalence of underweight women

Capacity Building and Support for Data Collection

As mentioned above, data will be obtained through assessments conducted by national statistical data collection units in the health and agricultural sectors. To assist Mali in developing strong and sustainable statistical systems, USG/Mali will build the capacity of the Ministry of Agriculture's CPS to conduct the LSMS-ISA, which will collect relevant and timely household-level agricultural data. USG/Mali will coordinate this capacity-building activity with the Permanent Households Surveys, led by INSTAT and supported by Statistics Sweden. These projects will collaborate with existing national surveys such as the Population and Household Census (RGPH), the Household Budget Survey (EBC), and the DHS to avoid duplication and to improve data collection capacity. Data from the LSMS-ISA, a five year project, will be fully documented and publicly disseminated 12 months after the completion of data collection each year. Demographic Health Surveys are also planned for Mali in 2011 and 2016. These surveys will serve as the baseline and end line surveys for Phase I of the Feed the Future initiative. USAID/Washington will support a mid-line survey through the FTF monitoring and evaluation central mechanism.

Impact Evaluations

In addition to a summary evaluation after the five-year endpoint of the USG/Mali Feed the Future program, a mid-term evaluation and specific impact evaluations will be conducted to learn from the program implementation outcomes and guide mid-term course adjustments. Summary and mid-term impact evaluations will be directed by the USG/Mali Program Office and conducted by independent third parties, while specific impact evaluations to assess selected interventions at the IR level will be directed by the AEG and Health teams, in collaboration with the implementing partners. The various data sources outlined above will be used in the impact evaluations and additional data collection undertaken as necessary. Scopes of work for external assessments or evaluations will require rigorous methodology and will be reviewed and approved by the USG/Mali Mission.

The Mission will also leverage non-Feed the Future funding to implement a learning agenda to better understand the root causes of malnutrition and the impact of specific interventions. Formative research on the root causes of anemia will be undertaken to inform anemia prevention and treatment interventions in the target areas. Additionally, consumer surveys will be used to understand social marketing coverage and utilization and inform communication strategies.

<u>Results Coordinating Committee</u>

USG/Mali will re-launch its Results Coordinating Committee (RCC). The RCC will be composed of a representative from each technical team and support office. They will be charged with ensuring implementation of USAID Forward's reform agenda in monitoring and evaluation, discussing best evaluative standards and practices, and tracking the Mission monitoring and evaluation system. The RCC will liaise with USAID/Washington and other partners to stay current on new developments, improve our internal systems, and better communicate results and lessons learned.

<u>Staffing for Monitoring and Evaluation</u>

The USG/Mali AEG office contains two highly qualified M&E specialists, one of them having more than 20 years of experience. In addition, the FTF will benefit from the support of the Health team's M&E Specialist as well the Mission M&E Officer based in the Program office.

6. FINANCIAL PLANNING

The Feed the Future strategy is aligned with Mali's CAADP approach and the PNIP-SA as its guiding principle for agricultural development. USG investments will align with and complement the GOM public sector contribution to the PNIP-SA. The total expenditure required for full implementation of the PNIP-SA is estimated at $755.42 million over a five-year time frame beginning in 2011 and lasting until 2015. This figure, which is based on costing simulations conducted by the CPS of the Ministry of Agriculture, was presented at the High-Level Regional CAADP Meeting for West Africa in Dakar, Senegal in June 2010. The GOM intends to pay for the investments proposed under the PNIP-SA through domestic and international sources. Domestic sources include an increased budget allocation from the GOM, cost recovery from the PNIP-SA, and private sector contributions. The PNIP-SA additionally calls for developing a greater number of public-private partnerships to reduce the cost of capital and stimulate market-oriented investments. The current funding gap for the PNIP-SA is estimated at $491.10 million. As an output from the CAADP Business Meeting in November 2010, USG/Mali has conducted a domestic resource costing study to better understand the funding gap and the GOM's capacity to encourage investment in its agricultural plan. The CPS of the Ministry of Agriculture assisted with the analysis, which will be presented to the PTF and the private sector in 2011.

Because of the integrated systems strengthening approach adopted by USG/Mali for its FTF strategy, it is very difficult to parse out investments by value chain and region. Most interventions in the enabling environment, for example, are cross-cutting and occur at the national level; they will affect multiple value chains to varying degrees. Likewise, investments in marketing support to rice farmers, for example, will benefit value chains across regions as their purpose is to integrate farmers from different geographical areas and specialties along the value chain.

USG/Mali will more closely coordinate its activities with other donors in the agricultural sector. The recently-launched $160 million PAPAM program funded by the World Bank, EU, IFAD and the Global Environment Facility Trust Fund will support the agricultural sector for the next six years. It provides a natural entry point for USG to collaborate in strengthening value chain actors' capacities in order to take advantage of market opportunities for the selected commodities. The level of contributions from other private sector actors, NGOs and civil society groups are not yet known, but expected contributions will be leveraged to sustainably develop systems to stimulate economic growth, improve nutritional outcomes, and raise household incomes. It will coordinate its credit guarantees with the $20 million FNAA (included in the PNIP-SA) and provide technical assistance to this mechanism in coordination with the World Bank. The $300 million, seven-year AGRA Breadbasket program is another mechanism into which program participants, banks, GOM, and donors are contributing to fulfill the PNIP-SA. USG/Mali will coordinate its investments with this program as well.

7. MANAGEMENT

The USG/Mali mission has suffered a shortage of staff and leadership in recent years. Thanks to efforts by the Africa Bureau and Human Resources, the mission will be fully staffed by fall 2011 and able to adequately manage the FTF program. The Mission Director will lead the Feed the Future program with technical support from the Accelerated Economic Growth, Health, Education, and Governance and Communications teams and the offices of Acquisition and Assistance and Financial Management. Within these teams, a core group of technical experts will lead coordination for the Feed the Future strategy.

A FSN nutrition specialist will be hired to join the core Feed the Future team in 2011 to provide management and technical support to the nutrition portfolio, act as a liaison between AEG and health, represent USG in donor coordination groups, and coordinate with the various GOM ministries that play a role in nutrition. The specialist may be jointly hired by the AEG and Health teams.

The USG/Mali technical offices will each contain representatives to coordinate their activities with that of the core Feed the Future management group, which consists of the AEG Team and the Nutrition members of the Health Team. In addition to nutrition specialists, the health team will also include specialists in malaria, maternal and child health, reproductive health and family planning, child survival and water and sanitation. These specialists will assist the core Feed the Future team on additional related health issues, such as sanitation, and hygiene. The Education team will contain a liaison to Feed the Future on issues related to out of school youth. The Governance and Communications team will coordinate its activities closely with Feed the Future.

A four-person Acquisition and Assistance staff that includes three A&A specialists will assist the core team in procurement and a four-person Financial Analyst Unit that will coordinate budgetary issues relating to Feed the Future. A six-person team from the Program Office, including one DLI, will assist in the coordination of all technical teams and support offices as they relate to Feed the Future.

In addition to the above USG/Mali staff, several external organizations have pledged their support to the Feed the Future program. The Economic Affairs Officer at the Department of State in Bamako will directly assist the core Feed the Future team to advocate for policies that will improve the business enabling environment. The most recent Peace Corps training group contains 62 volunteers that will be devoted to food security, split among core areas of Environment/Agriculture, Health Education, and Small Enterprise Development. The Ministry of Agriculture has pledged three full-time employees to coordinate government actions with the Feed the Future program.

8. ANNEXES

ANNEX A. WORLD BANK DOING BUSINESS, 2011

Doing Business Report 2011
Mali

REGION :	Sub-Saharan Africa
INCOME CATEGORY :	Low income
POPULATION :	13,010,209
GNI PER CAPITA (US$) :	680.00

DOING BUSINESS 2011 RANK	DOING BUSINESS 2010 RANK	CHANGE IN RANK
153	155	⬆2

TOPIC RANKINGS	DB 2011 Rank	DB 2010 Rank	Change in Rank
STARTING A BUSINESS	117	121	⬆4
DEALING WITH CONSTRUCTION PERMITS	87	91	⬆4
REGISTERING PROPERTY	88	98	⬆10
GETTING CREDIT	152	150	⬇-2
PROTECTING INVESTORS	147	146	⬇-1
PAYING TAXES	159	159	No change
TRADING ACROSS BORDERS	154	158	⬆4
ENFORCING CONTRACTS	133	135	⬆2
CLOSING A BUSINESS	106	116	⬆10

ANNEX B. LARGE MALIAN AGRIBUSINESS FIRMS

Agribusiness Private Sector in Mali – Illustrative Examples

Mali's agribusiness landscape is dominated by a handful of large agro-industrial companies, and thousands of small, medium-sized, and micro-enterprises operating at artisanal, semi-artisanal, or semi-industrial levels.

Large Agro-Industrials	Industry
Huilerie Cotonnière du Mali – Huicoma	Privatized cotton oil processing
Le Lido SA	Mineral water
Diago	Mineral water
Bramali	Brewery
Grands Moulins du Mali – GMM	Flour mill
Grand Moulin du Sahel	Flour mill
Groupe Industriel Madiou Simpara – GIMAS	Food and beverage production

SME Processors	Industry
Mam Cocktail	Local foods and juices production
UCODAL	Local foods production
Adja Transformation	Cereals processing, local foods production

ANNEX C. USG/MALI FEED THE FUTURE INTERVENTIONS

Value Chain Interventions

Each of the three selected value chains is embedded within a larger agricultural system and cannot be considered independently. Not only would a focus limited solely to the selected value chains be less effective in boosting production, it would also ignore opportunities to enhance incomes and increase access to nutritionally valuable foods. By working at the system level, USG/Mali FTF interventions will not only improve production, quality and market opportunities for rice, millet, sorghum and livestock, it will also increase availability and access to fish, cowpeas, dairy products and vegetables. Some of the interventions will have impacts in all three value chains; for example, building stronger farmer cooperatives and improving input supply, while others are specific to a particular system. Interventions range across the entire value chain, taking into account needs for boosting research, capacity building at both the local and the government levels, adopting improved technologies and management practices, private entrepreneurship, and improving the policy enabling environment.

Build Stronger Cooperatives and Farmer and Trader Organizations. USG/Mali will build the capacity of agricultural cooperatives (particularly women's cooperatives, including those in peri-urban areas), farmer and trader organizations, and inter-professional organizations that conduct critical coordination functions necessary for broad-based agricultural growth. USG/Mali-led partnerships will help build capacity to take on specific organizational development issues such as cooperative governance, financial management, business plan development and management. Community associations will be empowered to manage and maintain infrastructure investments such as those in water management for rice production or in cereal storage. Stronger organizations will help farmers to access credit, inputs, technology and technical know-how needed to improve productivity; to manage communal resources such as land, water and forage areas; and to obtain market information, improve quality, norms and standards and obtain higher prices for their products. Working effectively in this sector will depend on building effective partnerships with financial institutions, including microfinance and private entrepreneurs; local and international development partners; and other USG entities such as Peace Corps.

Boost the Quality of and Access to Agricultural Inputs. The low quality and limited availability of agricultural inputs in Mali, including seeds, fertilizer, and animal feed, limits crop yields and lowers animal health, thus constraining the amount and quality of food available at the household and national level and restricting farmers' abilities to earn more money from their products. To build a stronger seed sector, USG/Mali will partner with a variety of local organizations, research institutions and agribusiness dealers to improve the quality and quantity of inputs available. Partnerships with Afrique Verte, a local NGO, will promote seed fairs and address several deficiencies in the seed sector, including shortages of improved seeds available for purchase. Efforts to develop the nascent seed industry will include capacity building and entrepreneurship training, accompanied by policy reform efforts at the national level. Partnerships with IER will include developing their extension services to deliver technical assistance over a larger area in order to strengthen the monitoring capabilities of seed multipliers and to develop additional seed production capacity at the local level. USG/Mali will also partner with GOM extension agents and with the IPR to disseminate information on least cost animal rations that can help boost the weight and nutritional status of livestock.

Introduction of Best Agricultural Practices. The effectiveness of quality inputs can be maximized through the use of best agricultural practices that boost production and quality while reducing losses due to improper storage, pests, and other factors. USG/Mali will help to create better pathways for agricultural extension services – both public and private – to work directly with producer (especially women's) organizations to disseminate best practices on millet, sorghum, rice and livestock production. At the production level, this will involve improved management practices to conserve soil, retain moisture and reduce irrigation needs and will go hand in hand with scaling up Integrated Pest

Management (IPM) systems. For millet and sorghum specifically, USG /Mali partners will promote the use of soil and water management practices to stabilize yields and increase soil water retention. Some NRM activities will include soil anti-erosive actions, tied ridging, soil fertility improvement through composting and Assisted Natural Regeneration (ANR) of trees pioneered by NGOs and a USG tourism/NRM project in the Bankass *cercle* in the Mopti region.

Promote System Diversification through Intercropping and Rotations. Improved inputs and better management practices can increase production and quality and reduce post-harvest losses; however the sustainable intensification of Mali's agricultural systems can be greatly enhanced by the increasing the use of intercropping methods that have long been deployed in Mali. Intercropping cowpea, soy, and other legumes with millet and sorghum, and integrating horticulture and aquaculture into rice production systems can greatly increase overall system productivity. In addition to diversifying the diet, intercropping reduces the climate and market risk profiles of the primary agricultural product by improving soil fertility, thus reducing the need to purchase expensive fertilizers. These techniques have been extensively tested in local conditions and will be widely disseminated through extension programs, in conjunction with SBCC messaging. The result of this outreach will be to increase household consumption of a diverse array of foods to improve household nutritional status, especially among women and children. It provides an example of the opportunities to deliver holistic nutrition solutions through a "no missed opportunities" approach that couples SBCC with agricultural interventions.

Improve Access to Credit and Savings. Inadequate access to credit is a fundamental constraint inhibiting growth and development of the agricultural sector in Mali. Challenges include banks' inability to properly price risk, high default rates, high interest rates, and a predominance of short-term loans. Further, the most common cause for financial crisis within a Malian household is a critical health event; a clear linkage exists between health status and loan default rates. Technical assistance in finance will be provided to banks to more effectively manage and price their risk for agricultural endeavors across all value chains. Support will be provided to educate agro finance institutions as to the relationship between good health and loan repayment, and USG/Mali will look for opportunities to develop sustainable health education programs in financing mechanisms. Working through producer associations, USG/Mali will scale up warehouse receipt systems to guarantee contractual arrangements between producers, processors and exporters, and will develop savings schemes among farmer's groups at the producer association level. Livestock producers will also benefit from all of these advances because they will be able to purchase feed for their animals in order to fatten them and increase their price in the market.

Infrastructure Development and Improvement. USG/Mali will invest in small-scale infrastructure development to boost agricultural production and limit post-harvest losses. All infrastructure improvements or developments will be constructed at the village level for the communal use of all members of the collective or association and will be accompanied by activities to strengthen the ability of the association to manage the resource and any communal income generated. Their construction will build off of the recent successes of USG partners in constructing such facilities in accordance with local compacts where villagers supply labor and local materials for infrastructure developments while USG provides technical assistance and materials that cannot be locally procured.

USG/Mali will work with local communities to build, repair, or improve small-scale water management structures and irrigation facilities in the *bas fonds* of Sikasso, controlled flooding zones in Mopti, and irrigated perimeters in Timbuktu. *Bas-fonds* (inland lowland swamps) are currently largely undeveloped for rice production and are primarily cultivated by women, making them important for food security and women's incomes in southern Mali. Strengthening the ability of water users' associations to manage improvements to water and irrigation infrastructure is necessary for the sustainable operation of these investments. Reliable access to water and better water management will greatly increase and stabilize rice yields in these areas. Rice yields in irrigated perimeters can rise from a present 4.5 MT/ha to 6 MT/ha and in free flooding and small irrigation systems from 1.5 MT/ha to 2.5 MT/ha. Farmers in the millet, sorghum and rice value chains will benefit from 100 to 500 metric ton storage facilities for their crops. Improved storage facilities allow farmers to store food a longer period of time, thus reducing the necessity of having households purchase food on the open market when their provisions run out or are spoiled. In the livestock value chain, USG/Mali will build water access points for animals that travel the transhumant routes from the arid North to the subtropical South in order to improve their health before arriving at points where they can be exported or sold at a domestic market. Water access points will be developed in conjunction with improved pasture areas, both of which will be maintained by community organizations that will also control any user fees generated. A good example of how income can be created for women, particularly in small ruminants can be seen in the work of women's groups in small ruminant fattening enterprises. Interventions that would assist women's groups and other producers with the development of least cost rations and information on supplemental feed quality will optimize supplemental feeding for fattening and reduce overfeeding. Focusing livestock fattening in women's groups that are already selling supplemental feeds can increase incomes by reducing purchase of feeds from vendors or intermediaries.

Promote the Production and Marketing of Processed Products. USG/Mali will support a variety of interventions to promote the production and marketing of increasingly popular processed agricultural products as a means of adding value to transformed goods. Women are primarily affected by some processing activities like packaging sorghum and millet into more user-friendly configurations and by parboiling rice on the processing end by reaping income from their activities, and on the domestic end by reducing the amount of time they have to devote to household chores. To respond to these trends, USG/Mali will support the testing and demonstration of sorghum and millet processing and animal feed milling that depends on a rapid increase in the availability of uniformly clean millet and sorghum. First, producers will be connected to processors through contractual arrangements designed to secure a consistent supply of quality agricultural commodity products at a stable price. Second, technical assistance will be extended to processors to develop value-added products that respond to consumer preferences. USG/Mali will target large processors to forge links with farmer organizations to ensure a stable supply of quality product. It will also target several small-scale milling enterprises that already work with farmer organizations in several zones, including in Sikasso, Mopti and Timbuctu. Where possible, fortification will be used with value-added processing to strengthen the nutritional content. Parallel work at the national level to ensure fortification regulations are enforced will make this practice more widespread.

Improving the Enabling Environment for Agriculture and Nutrition

Policy Reforms in the Agriculture Enabling Environment. USG/Mali will remain firmly engaged in policy debates in order to help the GOM avoid backsliding into policies that have proven detrimental to agricultural growth and food security. Policy engagement will focus on a number of issues central to the enabling environment such as trade barriers, fertilizer and seed policy, interest rate subsidies, land policy, the legal framework, and contract enforcement. USG/Mali will work with the Department of State to encourage biosafety and SPS that are expected to contribute to increased exports. Expanding ongoing coordination with USG/WA on regional trade corridors through the West Africa Trade Hub will also encourage regional exports and expand new markets for products. Strengthening ongoing cooperation on intellectual property rights regimes with the CLDP will also boost the prospects to attract private investment, primarily in the seed sector. Work with the commerce, tax, and customs offices, in partnership with the World Bank, will help rural and unregistered small and medium agricultural enterprises move into the formal sector. The World Bank and IMF will play a leading role in macroeconomic reforms, conducted in close coordination and cooperation with the PTF, in which USG plays an active role.

Nutrition Policy and Advocacy. USG /Mali's FTF nutrition strategy will support GOM offices, policies, and strategies that will advance the government's capacity to promote and coordinate nutrition interventions at the national level. First, USG/Mali will promote nutrition as an elevated cross-cutting issue in GOM ministries, an essential measure given the complex nature of nutritional outcomes in Mali. USG/Mali will continue to work with other donors and partners to support an elevated inter-sectoral nutrition office in the GOM that can effectively promote and coordinate nutrition policy. Through the SUN process, USG/Mali will continue to support the GOM as needed in collaboration with other donors. Second, USG/Mali will continue to provide technical support to the Ministry of Health to reevaluate its ten-year health strategy and to plan for the next five years with a stronger emphasis on the role of nutrition in health. Finally, USG/Mali will support the GOM to formulate and pass industrial food-based fortification legislation that regulation should also promote future investment in this important agro-food activity.

<u>Training and Building the Capacity of the Government, Private Sector, and NGOs</u>

Capacity building will be incorporated into almost every activity taking place under Feed the Future to ensure the sustainability of institutions and policies that USG/Mali will be supporting.

1. Agriculture and Nutrition Education and Knowledge Management

Strengthen Agricultural Education. USG /Mali will support agricultural education at all levels, from basic adult literacy, through technical and managerial training, to agricultural higher education. It is necessary, however, to coordinate with the Mission's Education team and with other donors, as it will be very difficult and costly to rapidly transform the agricultural sector when a large part of the rural population is illiterate. The USG/Mali AEG and Education teams are partnering on an initiative to teach agricultural entrepreneurship skills to out of school youth; in this program, basic literacy and numeracy will be delivered along with best practices in processing and cultivation techniques. Technical training for producers and local operators will take place at the community organization level and will be integrated with value chain interventions. USG /Mali will strengthen agricultural vocational schools and technical institutes, particularly the University of Bamako and IPR, to help meet the anticipated increase in demand for a new generation of agricultural technicians and extension agents, both public and private by developing curriculums. International research partnerships also provide opportunities for Malian students to obtain PhD and Master degrees at U.S. universities while at the same addressing pressing research needs in Mali.

Improved Knowledge Management and Dissemination. Improving the transmission of knowledge is a fundamental primary step to bolstering Mali's capacity to move from an agriculture-based economy centered on internal trading and resource extraction to one that is environmentally sustainable and capable of generating the productivity increases necessary to support improved rural incomes and agricultural transformation.

Strengthening the capacity of Malians to tap into the enormous wealth of scientific knowledge now available in the world and adapt it to Mali's conditions is one of the two basic challenges facing Malian agriculture. Although the GOM sponsors several organizations that collect agricultural data like INSTAT, the CPS, customs, and the meteorological services, the information collected is often not analyzed in a way that fosters efficient decision-making processes, particularly for the cereals market. This creates problems in times of crisis, when the analysis of unclear and diffuse data triggers severe policy responses like export bans. In response to this issue, USG /Mali will expand on a pilot program to create a cell phone-based method of collecting and sharing critical information, such as grain inventory levels in local cereal banks at the commune level. This data will feed into a central database that will be available to national and sub-national leaders. USG /Mali will also work with the World Bank to introduce the LSMS-ISA to the CPS in the Ministry of Agriculture to build capacity within the CPS and furnish accurate local-level information to both national and local policy-makers. Fostering a culture of improved governance is the second basic step that is necessary to create an incentive structure to use this knowledge productively.[50] The political pressure on analysts who make recommendations about agricultural development to political decision-makers must be reduced in a context of increased reliance on agriculture as a means toward development. USG /Mali will examine the factors that have fostered the creation of independent non-partisan think thanks in sub-Saharan Africa in particular with a view of support the emergence of a few in Mali.

Agricultural Extension and Advisory Services. Agricultural extension and advisory services in Mali are fragmented, understaffed, underfunded and have limited reach. Government services are offered through several different Ministries and further divided along crop lines and by geographical regions. USG /Mali's approach will be to work to sustainably strengthen the ability of the government institutions to provide improved extension and advisory services while simultaneously exploring new models to facilitate transferring this role to agribusiness dealers, processors and other private sector players. USG /Mali recently commissioned an initial scoping mission by the Modernizing Extension and Advisory Services Project (MEAS), a project managed by the USAID/BFS, which will be followed by a more in-depth assessment to guide future interventions. Further work under this project will help design interventions to sustainably rebuild, and possibly inform the restructuring of, the GOM extension services. These efforts will keep in mind the limitations inherent to the government system while recognizing that alternative providers, such as the private sector, will simply not reach all of the target producers. USG/Mali will assist private agribusiness dealers to build partnerships with associations and cooperatives to improve access to inputs and appropriate scale farm machinery. They will also to serve as an alternative source of relevant technical information on production, storage, processing and quality standards. Additionally, USG/Mali will work with these businesses to cross train their agents in situationally appropriate health education and nutrition messages as a part of the "no missed opportunities" approach to SBCC

Improved Health Information and Logistics Systems. Under GHI, the USG/Mali Health team provides on-going technical assistance to strengthen and support the health information management system in Mali as well as logistics management systems. Both are critical to improving nutritional status. The health information management system provides the GOM and stakeholders data on the nature and severity of health problems, as well as the nature and quality of the services being delivered to ill individuals. Logistics management systems assure that food supplements are available along with other necessary supplies to treat ill individuals seeking care at local health clinics. Illustrative examples of technical assistance include revising of data collection tools, facilitating supervision to review the quality of data and service delivery, and quantification exercises to predict the amount and type of commodities that facilities need to ensure that they have enough stock to treat ill individuals.

Health Extension Services/Health Systems Strengthening. Under GHI and in conjunction with FTF, USG/Mali will equip and train two levels of health extension workers in a variety of health services, including SBCC on Essential Nutrition Actions (ENA) and other healthy behaviors that affect nutritional status such as vaccination, family planning, and ante natal care. Volunteer health workers (*relais*) also sell health commodities to the community, and will be provided initial stock and education on point-of-use water treatment kits, and zinc-fortified oral rehydration salts, and selected other products. The level II *relais*, or community health agents, are a new cadre of health worker with enough training to provide more extensive services outside of health facilities. This cadre will be rolled out during the FTF timeframe in the targeted regions; USG/Mali will support the training of these workers on CMAM, ENA, iron/folate supplementation and other key nutrition services. These two cadres of health workers

---

[50] MSU 2011

constitute the primary point of contact that most Malians have with the formal health system, and as such will be the primary platform to deliver SBCC messages to mothers.

2. Agriculture Research

Agricultural research is a fundamental part of value chain investment strategies and provides the basis for the introduction and adaptation of new innovations to enhance productivity, processing, storage and marketing. Investments will require building the capacity of Malian agricultural research institutions to adapt existing technologies or undertake new research of relevance to agricultural systems in Mali. They will also require building stronger links between research institutions and pathways of technology dissemination and adoption, to include the public extension system, but also via novel delivery mechanisms involving the private sector, NGOs, or farmer cooperatives. Ongoing consultations with the private sector will introduce a demand-driven approach to technology generation and dissemination, as investments will speak to the needs that the private sector identifies.

Adapting Management Practices to Target Environments. USG/Mali will emphasize adapting and disseminating best environmental management practices that conserve water, build soil health, and reduce labor needs while also increasing productivity. USG/Mali will also fine-tune systems for intercropping and crop rotations, involving evaluating rice, millet and sorghum varieties that are shorter duration or have other characteristics to better integrate them into diverse cropping systems. Evaluating resource conserving technologies within the context of the entire cropping system is important. Local adaptation of best practices in pasture management will also be necessary as watering holes are built and community organizations gain the ability to manage them and associated pasture areas. The principle organizations through which USG /Mali will partner are IER, IPR, producer associations, and agricultural cooperatives in our target communes.

Improved Genetics of Crop Varieties and Livestock. Improving the genetic material used in the production of crops and livestock is another important research area. USG/Mali will partner with WASA, INTSORMIL, and with IPR to adapt millet, sorghum, and rice seeds to local conditions, especially as they relate to water use efficiency and drought tolerance. It will also build the capacity of research institutions like IPR to manage biotech crop adaptation as projects developing insect-resistant cowpea, and drought-tolerant and fertilizer use efficient rice move into product evaluation. Supporting IPR work to genetically improve the livestock value chain (including improved breeds of cattle, goat, and sheep, and improved forage crops) can increase weight gain in animals, and thus farmer productivity, without significantly changing herder practices or risk profiles. Scaling-up the production of animal vaccines is another focus of USG/Mali's partnership with IPR.

3. Nutrition Research

Improving Anemia Prevention and Control Programs. Using a quality improvement methodology at small scale, FTF will look at whether or not better coverage of existing services will lower anemia rates. The outcome of this operational research will be used to determine the nature of the intervention that is needed to address anemia, which will then be scaled up using the government health system and partners.

ANNEX D. FEED THE FUTURE RESULTS FRAMEWORK

Feed the Future Results Framework – USAID/Mali 2011-2015

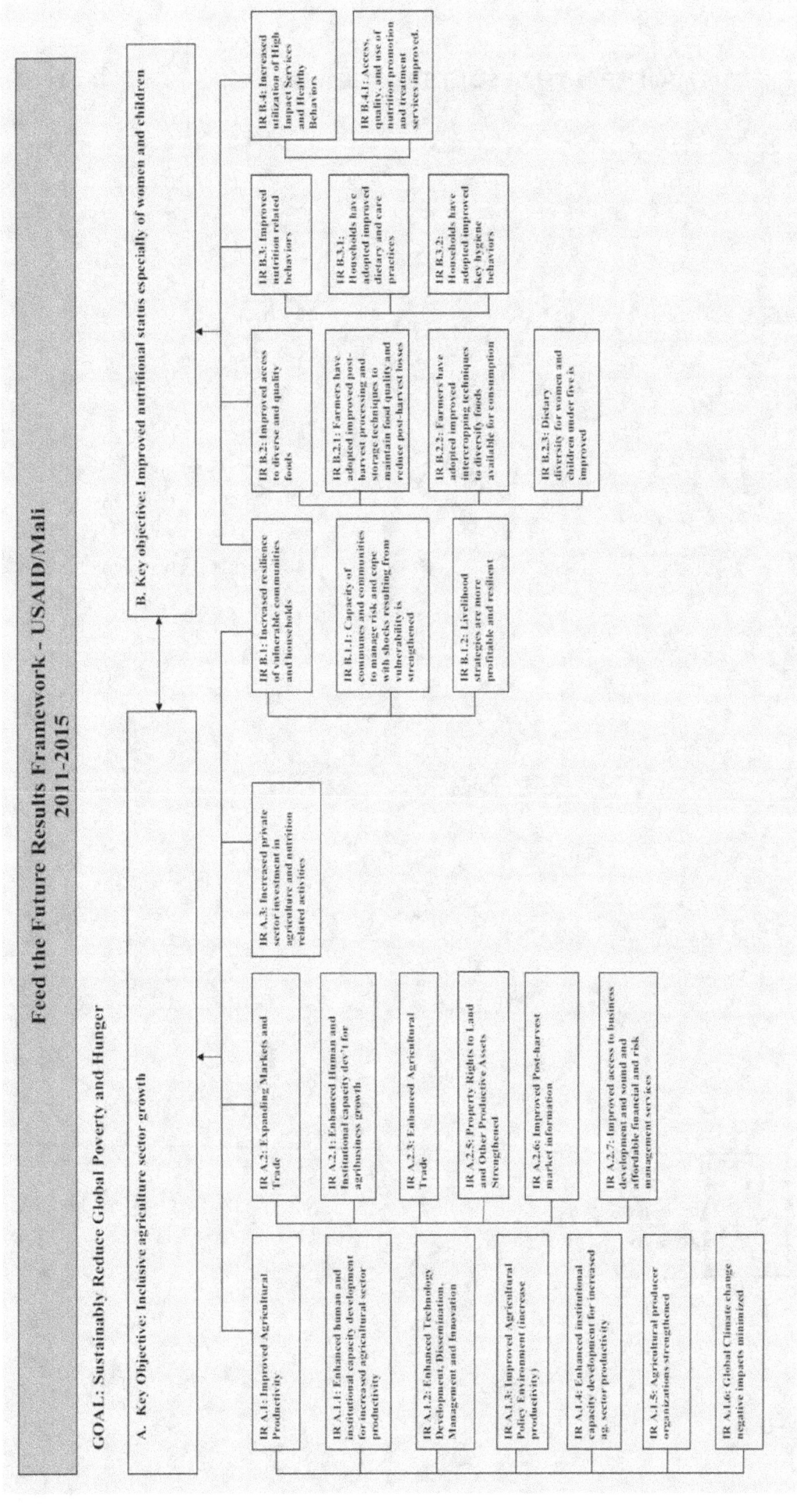

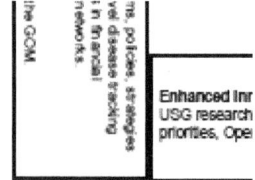

Donor	Programs & Description	Possible Areas to Leverage Resources
WFP	***Purchase for Progress:*** $1.7M/2 year program that provides alternate market outlets favorable to smallholder farmers.	- Link sorghum and millet farmers to WFP market opportunities - Capacity building of producer organizations
AGRA	***Breadbasket Initiative:*** $122M-$156M program aimed at improving the grain ecosystem of Sikasso by working across the rice, corn, and sorghum value systems. Considering expansion into other FtF areas.	- Seed system development (production, policy, and distribution chain) - Development of warehousing systems - Access to credit - Capacity development of producer organizations and aggregated farms - Market development and linkages
GIZ & KFW	***Programme National d'Irrigation de Proximité (PNIP):*** Provides a national federating framework for all small irrigation projects.	- Employ project's existing financing and contracting mechanism for the construction and rehabilitation of small irrigation systems and for the development of local infrastructure management committees
World Bank, European Union, Global Fund, IFAD	***Programme d'Appui au Productivité Agricole au Mali (PAPAM):*** $160M/6-year program aiming to increase productivity of agricultural and agribusiness producers in select production systems.	- Expansion of lowland rice irrigation (Sikasso) - Cereals production and marketing (Mopti, Sikasso) - Small ruminant fattening (Mopti, Sikasso) - Facilitating rural credit development - Capacity development to producer organizations and strengthening of the agricultural extension system - Support to sector monitoring and evaluation
Danish Embassy	***PASAM:***	- Collaborative work on studies; topics include private sector demand, packaging, and public sector support to the agricultural sector, agriculture and value chains assessments
European Union	***Climate Change and Food Security Programs.*** The US and EU have committed to strengthen collaboration in these two areas, and in the achievement of MDGs. Mali is one of "pilot countries" to begin implementing cooperation in Food Security, and in climate change adaptation.	- Discussions are underway at the country level - One example of area of potential collaboration: EU currently provides funding to ICRISAT to support work on millet/sorghum - See PAPAM program above
UNICEF	***Nutrition:*** Leading the implementation activities and scale up of interventions in the management and treatment of acute malnutrition; also supports Ministry of Health in policy, strategy development, advocacy, development of production and advocacy materials.	- Leading effort with USG to develop a nutrition donor collaboration group to improve collaboration, leveraging and coordinating interventions in this area

Above is an illustrative list of concrete opportunities that USG has identified for leveraging FTF resources with other donors, and which are currently under discussion.

USG is also presently working with the Danish Embassy (Leader of the Rural Economy PTF Group) to map the landscape of major donor programs and projects in the domain of agriculture and food security. Below is a rough and illustrative listing of donor areas which overlap with the FTF program and which USG may explore for collaboration or joint-funding opportunities:

Donor	Potential Areas of Collaboration
African Development Bank	• Rice (Mopti) • Cattle (Sikasso) • Small Ruminants (Sikasso) • Fish (Mopti, Timbuktu) • Seeds, M/S (Mopti) • Dairy (Sikasso)
Belgium Coop	• Chef de Fille for Livestock • Livestock (Mopti) • Involved in Fish (Sikasso, Mopti) • Dairy (Mopti)
BOAD	• Involved in Cattle
CECI (Canada)	• Involved In Rice
FAO	• Livestock • Rice
France (ADF)	• Involved in Rice
Japan (JICA)	• Small ruminants • Fish (Mopti) • Rice (Timbuktu, Mopti)
Luxembourg	• Involved in cattle and small ruminants
Netherlands Cooperation	• Involved in Rice (Mopti)
Netherlands Embassy	• Experiences, activities, and instruments in private sector support/PPPs
ONUDI	• Involved in Dairy • Cattle (Timbuktu) • Small Ruminants (Timbuktu) • Fish (Timbuktu)
Swiss Contact	• Involved in Rice; markets and trade dev't
United Nations/Spain	• Implementation of Initiative 166, which aims to accelerate MDGs in 166 communes through an integrative program, is being funded in certain communes of Mopti by Spanish (the « Bandiagara Initiative»)

ANNEX G. FEED THE FUTURE ANALYSIS SIKASSO REGION MAP

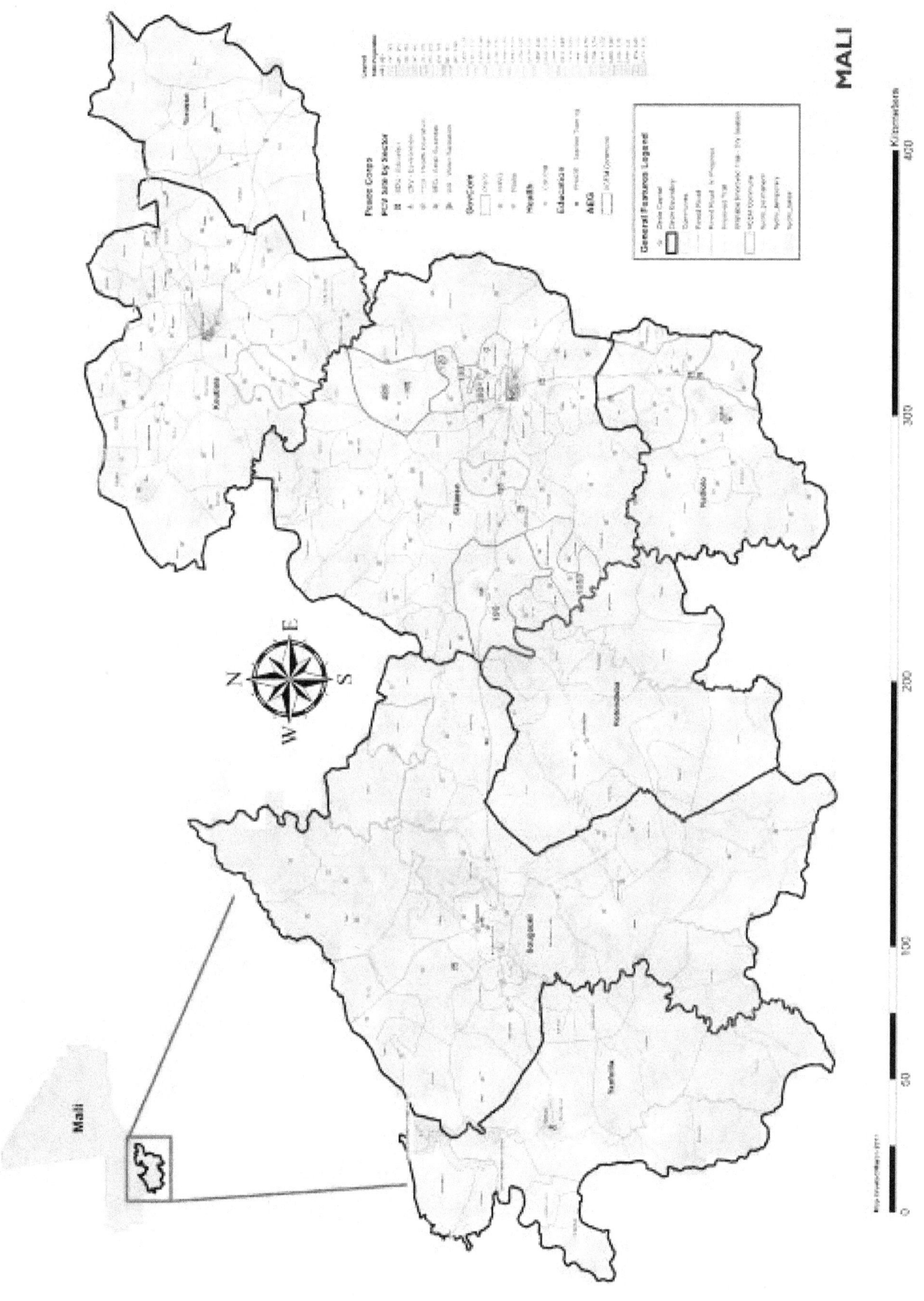

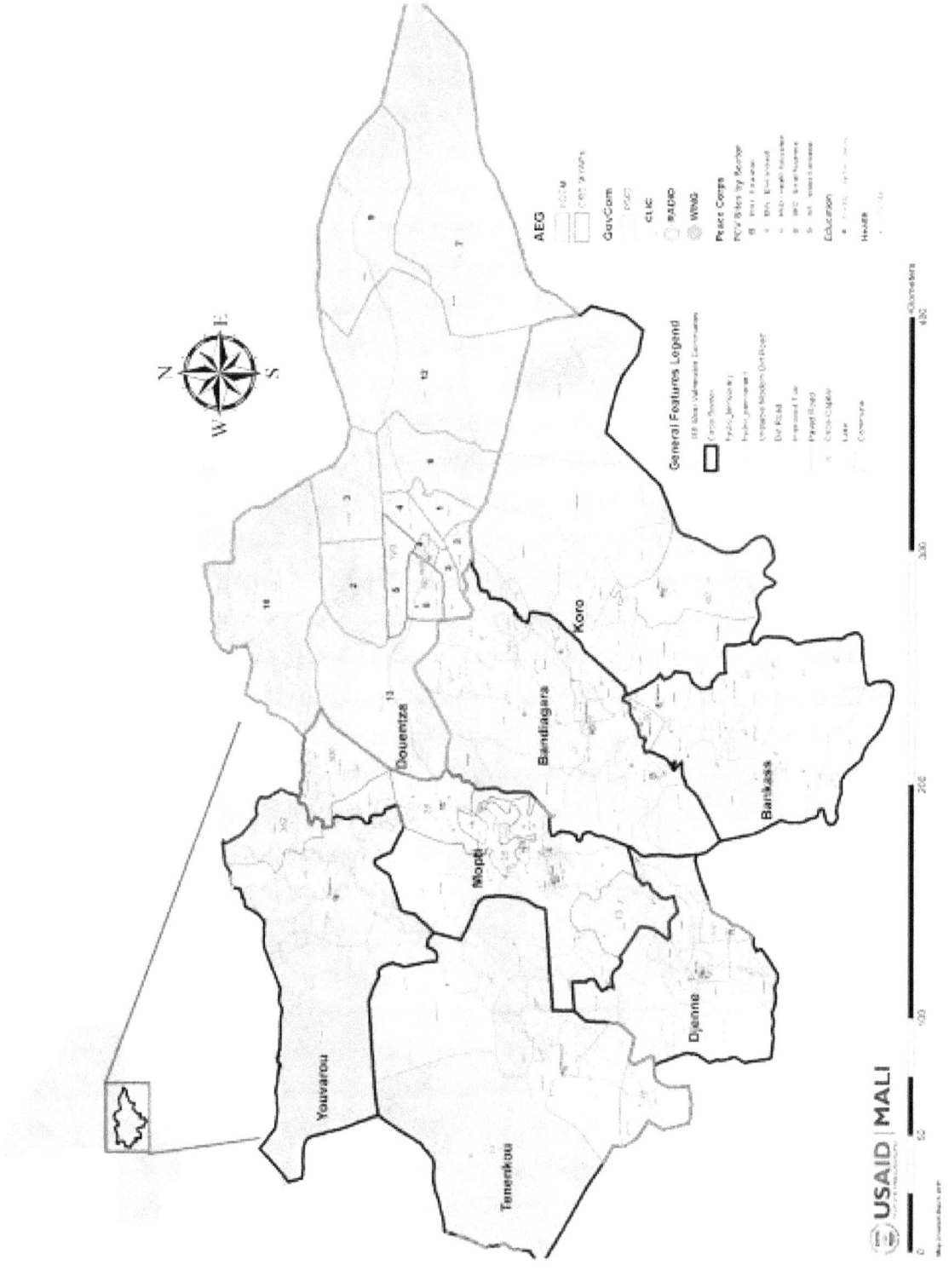

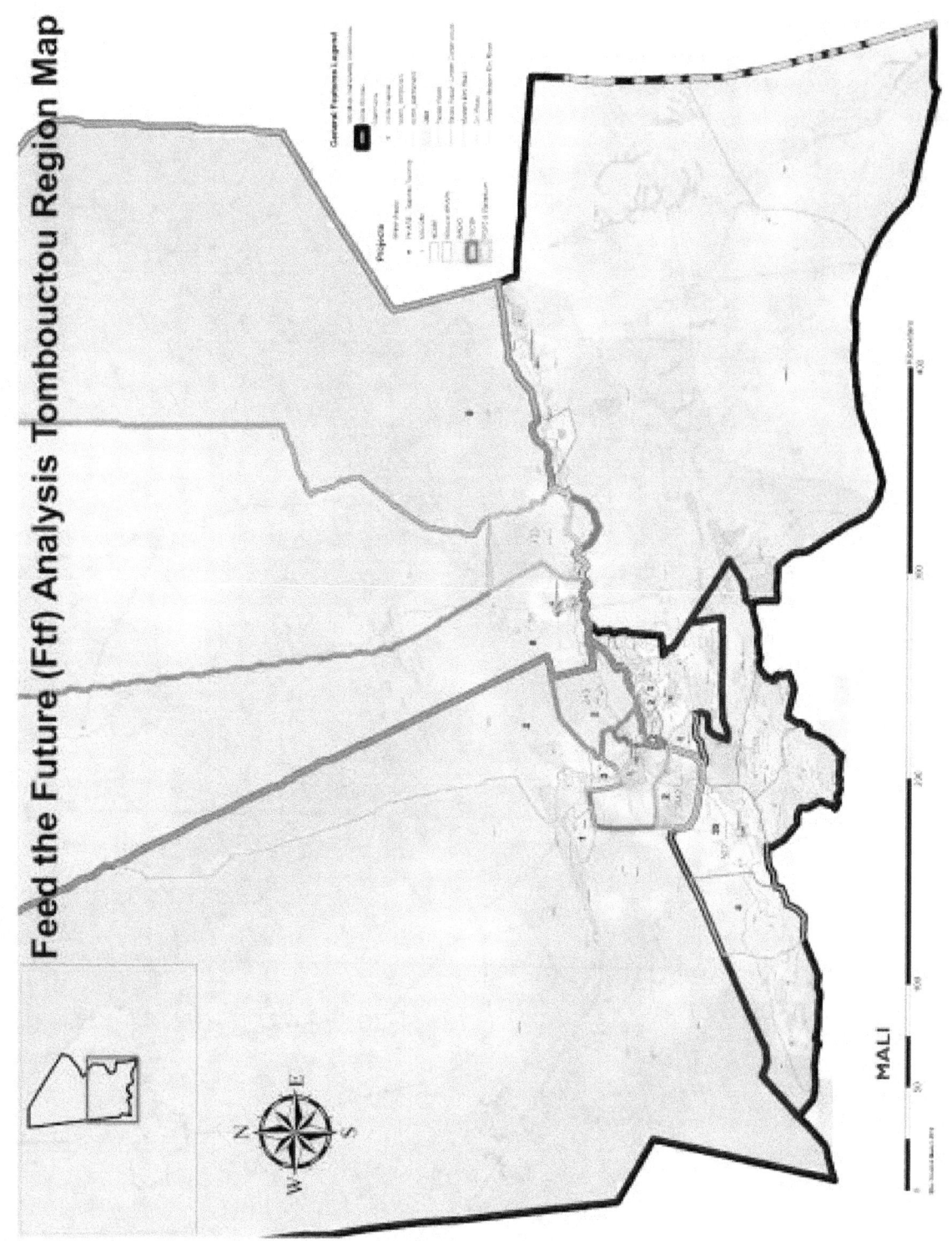

Feed the Future (Ftf) Analysis Tombouctou Region Map